A LANDMARK OPERATIVE FREE MASONRY

WRITTEN TO COMMEMORATE
THE CENTENARY OF
'THE OPERATIVES'

DAVID KIBBLE-REES

(Cover photograph taken in Tintern Abbey,
an 11th century landmark in operative masonry).

Other Lulu publications by the same Author

The Operatives (2006)

An Introduction to the Commemorative Masonic Order of St Thomas of Acon (2008)

Which way do I go from here? (2010)

©
2013

CONTENTS	PAGE
Introduction	5
Events leading up to May 1913	10
The first fifty years (1913-1963)	29
Consolidation and expansion (1964-2013)	56
Some distinguishing characteristics of the Society	69
The Grand Master Masons	85
A toast to the Founders	91
Appendix A The Grand Master Masons	95
Appendix B Principal Grand Officers	100
Appendix C The Regions	104
Appendix D The Assemblages	120
Appendix E Order of Service to Operative Masonry	126
Index	127

The 1st Grand Master Mason

Rt. W. Bro. Nigel Alan Willows VIIº

INTRODUCTION

This book has been written to celebrate the one hundredth anniversary of a society which was founded in 1913 and has since become known throughout the masonic world as 'The Operatives', although its real name is The Worshipful Society of Free Masons, Rough Masons, Wallers, Slaters, Paviors, Plaisterers and Bricklayers.

As a society it evolved from one small initiative on the part of a certain Clement Edwin Stretton who, as Secretary of the York Division of Operative Free Masons and the man who breathed new life into two moribund lodges of operative free masons in Leicestershire, took it upon himself to authorise the opening of a London Section of those lodges in order to extend his self-imposed task of perpetuating the ceremonies, traditions and language of the ancient Guild operative masons. Both of the Leicestershire lodges disappeared soon after his death, but the London Section has remained in existence ever since, albeit under a different name (i.e. Channel Row Assemblage) and has steadily grown to become the world-wide Society that it is today.

Stretton's reason for reviving the two lodges in Leicestershire and authorising a London Section was his firm conviction that Guild operative masons were the forerunners of modern speculative freemasonry. To be more precise, it was their ceremonies which had been hijacked in 1717 and watered-down by the Reverend Dr. James Anderson (1680-1739), whose name is forever linked with the early days of the Premier Grand Lodge of England and digesting the old Constitutions of freemasonry into "a new and better method". Stretton's view was that this was something which ought to be known and acknowledged by all speculative freemasons, many of whom were unaware of the origins of their fraternity. Some, in fact, in what one writer tactfully described as "knowledgeable quarters", were beginning to challenge *any* idea that linked speculative freemasonry to the ancient stonemasons and, in the absence of undeniable evidence to substantiate those claims, were beginning to look elsewhere for the origins of speculative freemasonry, such as in "the religious troubles of the post-Elizabethan period when a network of secret societies may have adopted the trappings of operative masonry as a disguise and shield"[1]. Expressed briefly, it was Stretton's intention to disabuse them of those and other ideas, in favour of the claims of the Operatives.

Whether he was right in all, or even in part, of that which he claimed, or whether he foresaw the growth of the society which would result from his initiative, is beyond consideration in this book, which is only intended to form a part of the Society's centenary celebrations. It is, however, hoped that it will, at the same time, satisfy a need, long felt by its members, for a history of the Society for the benefit of those who are already members, and those who may wish to join in the future. Until now, apart from an interim history published in 2006, the Society has never possessed such a thing; not because it wasn't justified, but because of the scarcity of reliable evidence to support it. The unfortunate fact is that the original Guild masons committed little to writing and when one job finished, they simply shut-up shop and moved on to another leaving little, if anything, behind them in the form of documentary evidence. This, of course, may have been for any number of reasons, such as a desire to respect whatever Obligations they had taken when joining the Guild; because of the low-level of adult literacy in those days; or to ensure their safety from arrest and imprisonment during the years when the Combination Acts were in force. So, in that connection, it is probably worth adding that finding corroborative primary evidence to support each and every word contained in this book has proved difficult, and further complicated by a combination of two World Wars; occasional fires; thoughtlessness on the part of some of its members; records being thrown away by the Executors of senior members of the Society who died 'in office'; and the fact that, until recently, the Society has never had a headquarters of its own wherein such records could be deposited. All of which hopefully serves to explain why much of what follows is based on secondary evidence, i.e. obtained from the writings of others, some of whom were contemporaries of Stretton. This is not to say that there is anything inherently wrong with secondary evidence. It just doesn't carry the weight of those primary sources preferred, and held to be more credible, by academic historians. For better or worse therefore, and until some hitherto undiscovered archive of primary resource material unexpectedly comes to light to remedy the situation, this is the most complete history of the Society currently possible.

      Three points needs to be clarified before concluding this Introduction, the first of which is that although the modern Operatives recall or replicate whatever they have been able to discover of the ceremonies, procedures and language of the ancient Guild operative masons, they make no claim to be their linear successors. After withering away for years, Guild operative free masonry faded into history in the late 19th century, although some would date it much earlier than that. The modern Operatives merely hope they are preserving something of their ritual and customs, because they believe they were the fountainhead of modern speculative freemasonry and provide insight into much that is said and done in lodges today.

Secondly, throughout this book readers will encounter words which might appear misspelled or misquoted, such as antient, free mason, paviors or plaisterers, so it is necessary to explain in advance that they are not mistakes, but simply a personal preference for the spelling of those being quoted. For example, the operative free masons had their reasons for using two words (i.e. free mason) as distinct from the single word (freemason) used by speculative masons today. It is hoped that the practice will not prove distractive..

Finally, it is considered necessary to point out that in this book readers are likely to encounter certain passages similar to others they encountered in my interim history of the Society published in 2006. That having been said, they are reminded that in the Preface to that book, it was explained that that publication was only a stepping-stone on the way to the centenary of the Society in 2013, when a detailed history would be published. This book, therefore, is the final stage in a process which began seven years ago. All I can add by way of explanation is that, during the interim period, a certain amount of new information has come to light, and some of my earlier views have become modified. I can only hope that the modifications resulting from those changes will justify the publication of this final version of the Society's history.

David Kibble-Rees   January 2013

REFERENCE

1   Seal-Coon, F. W. 'An old-time Operative Midsummer Ceremony' in *Ars Quatuor Coronatorum* Vol. 105. p. 161

CHAPTER 1

Events leading up to May 1913

In the early part of the 20th century a locally well-known freemason from Leicester decided to promote the case for Guild operative free masons to be acknowledged - once and for all - as the fountainhead of speculative freemasonry. Operative free masonry, it should be explained, was concerned with the shaping and finishing of stones for use in the construction of castles, cathedrals and similar structures, whereas speculative freemasonry is concerned with the betterment of man, and only uses stones and stonemasons' tools to explain philosophical ideas by way of moral lessons and allegories. The former has existed from time immemorial, whereas speculative freemasonry is a by-product of the Enlightenment and can only be traced to the 17th or 18th centuries, depending on which theory one chooses to accept. It had once been regarded as axiomatic that one had grown out of the other but, towards the end of the 19th century, there were more than a few who were beginning to challenge that view.

By the time he made his decision most lodges and quarries which, at one time or another, had been operated along Guild lines had already faded into history but, in 1717, when speculative freemasonry is said to have begun, they had existed for hundreds of years, as explained by masonic historians, such as Harry Carr[1],

Harry Leroy Haywood[2] and Bernard E. Jones[3]. It is also evident from documents such as the Regius Manuscript, the date of which is estimated at 1390, which contains rules and regulations for the government of a Guild of craftsmen; and the Harleian Manuscript, which refers "to characters and Constitutions of Chester Companies and Guilds of the seventeenth century"[4]. The influence of Guilds, it was said, had for centuries permeated every aspect of daily life, whether spiritual, economic or social and, to quote just two examples, to this day many Local Authorities are still administered from 'Guild Halls'; and England's greatest writer, Shakespeare, is known to have attended a school in Stratford-upon-Avon which was, and still is, described as a 'Guild school'.

The Guildhall in the City of London

The freemason who made the decision to promote the claims of Guild operative free masonry was a Civil Engineer and author by the name of Clement Edwin Stretton and, according to one of his biographers, he was educated at the Rugby school made famous by Thomas Hughes and his "home background was a privileged one of the middle class"[5]. His father was successively a Councillor, Magistrate, Alderman, and Mayor of Leicester, and head of a firm of solicitors which he started himself; and it says something about his strength of character that in the late 19th century he became known at a national level for his implacable opposition to compulsory vaccination against smallpox. In fact, so vehement was his opposition that it resulted in his refusing, as a Magistrate, to deal with cases brought under the Vaccination Acts of the 19th century. They were a proud family and, according to a Leicester City Council's website, were "descended from the ancient family of Stretton seated at Leire, Co. Leic., in the reign of Henry VIII".

Like his father, Stretton became active in speculative freemasonry, mainly at a local level in Leicester, and gradually worked his way through the various grades of Craft (in St. John's Lodge No. 279), Royal Arch (in Chapter of Fortitude No. 279), Mark (in Simon de Montfort Lodge No. 194) and the Red Cross of Constantine (in Byzantine Conclave No. 44), eventually attaining the rank of Provincial Senior Grand Warden and gaining a reputation as a masonic historian, for public speaking, and for arranging visits to places of local interest, such as those he arranged to a quarry for Granite Lodge No. 2028 in 1908, and to a brewery, for Grace Dieu Lodge No. 2428 in 1909.

It is not intended to burden readers further by repeating in full the circumstances under which he became involved in Guild free masonry, which is readily available elsewhere[6,7], and it is hoped that it will be sufficient to briefly explain that he was first admitted into a Guild lodge in Derbyshire, when he was sent there in his youth to gain some experience of stonemasonry as part of his training to become an Engineer. Engineering at that time, it should be explained, was not a distinct profession and there was no direct method of entry by way of university. Moreover, whatever professional organizations existed (e.g. the Society of Civil Engineers or the Institute of Mechanical Engineers) were still in their infancy.

In any event, thereafter, he pursued a career in engineering, but did so with two additional interests. One was the railways about which he wrote over a hundred books and pamphlets, and regularly appeared in Court as an expert witness on matters of railway safety; and the other was freemasonry, in which he made constant progress, both in speculative freemasonry (as explained above) and in Guild free masonry, which he always claimed was superior to, and more complete than, speculative freemasonry. Although never actually employed as a stonemason, during more than forty years' involvement with the Guild, he gradually worked his way through all seven degrees of their system until he finally became a Senior Passed Master, 3rd Master Mason and, eventually, Secretary of the York Division, which was one of eight Guild Divisions covering the whole of England and Wales. Those eight Divisions had been delineated at a General Assembly held at Masons' Hall, London, on 30th November 1677, as explained in papers by Stretton and his contemporaries[8] and, more recently, by Neville Barker Cryer[9], the other Divisions being: (1) City of London (2) Westminster (3) Southern (4) Bristol (5) Chester (6) Isle of Anglesey and (7) Lancaster.

According to Bernard Dat[10], Stretton's strategy for promoting the claims of the Guild operatives had four elements. One was by writing about his beliefs to local newspapers, such as the *Melton Mowbray Times*, the *Coalville Times*, and the *Stafford Advertiser*, and submitting articles and letters to masonic publications, such as the *Freemason,* the *Free-masons' Chronicle*, and the *Co-mason* (later renamed the *Speculative Mason)*. Another was by conducting a lively correspondence with like-minded researchers and authors, especially those he considered able and willing to assist him in his cause. The third element was to give lectures concerning his beliefs, and to encourage others to do likewise. One of his own talks (*Tectonic Art. Ancient Trade Guilds and Companies*) given to the Leicester Association of Engineers in 1909, proved so popular that it was reprinted for sale (at a cost of one shilling) by the *Melton Mowbray Times*. The fourth element was to revive two former Guild lodges (i.e. Leicester Lodge No 91 and Mount Bardon Lodge No. 110), one with the intention of working the old Guild ceremonies, and the other to act as a base for a Correspondence Circle with the object of enrolling anyone who expressed an interest in, or desire to become involved with, Guild Operative free masonry. Both lodges were based at the granite quarries in Bardon which, as a village, has now almost totally disappeared under a Business Park near Exit 22 off the M1 motorway, a few miles east of Coalville. Nearly all traces of the two lodges have also disappeared, but a 1907 list of the members of one of them (i.e. Mount Bardon Lodge No. 110) was fortunately preserved and published by the Rev. R.R.à-Ababrelton, a former Grand Clerk of the Society, for his *Operative Review for December 1941*, and reads as follows:

1. John Yarker
2. Clement Edwin Stretton
3. Robert Bennett Grant
4. John Alfred Grant
5. Robert Walter Grant
6. William George M. Bailey
7. Frank Thos. Bellward
8. John Martin
9. Geoffrey W.F. Bellward
10. Percy E. Ogden
11. Harry Edgar Bann
12. Thomas Frith
13. Eli Parsons
14. Henry Harris
15. B.F.Stretton
16. A.Bowes
17. L.C.Smith
18. Thos. W. Thornton
19. Edward Peacock Smale
20. J.E.Morcambe
21. Richard Pride
22. Chas. W. Rossell
23. Thomas Carr
24. E.Beckwith
25. Richard C. Harrison
26. J.T.Joy
27. Nathan Harrison
28. John G. Purser
29. V. Lehmann
30. Karl Lauer
31. C.B.De Malmedy
32. John A. Sherren
33. S. Clifton Bingham
34. George Henry Grant
35. A. Gorham
36. Walter S. Hildesley
37. Harmon Kunfully Krad
38. William O. Wellsford
39. Charles Francis Bridge
40. Isaac Henry Vrooman Jnr.
41. Frederick William White
42. William Lane Gillespie
43. Henry E. Richards
44. Peter G.T. Eycte
45. Jared S. Horton
46. William H. Gladding
47. Charles E. Davis
48. James T. Barker

49. Wm. C. Gloeckner	50. Romey H. Brooks
51. Jesse A. White	52. Edwin Potts
53. Harry Smith	54. William Hammond
55. J. George Gibson	56. W.H. Hallsworth
57. Charles Hope Merz	58. Lewis M. Lea
59. Frank H. Marquis	60. James J. Davey
61. Fred J. Brier	62. Jas M. de May
63. W.H. Spencer Strong	64. Augustus L. Moss
65. John T. Mack	66. Charles E. Stroud
67. Harry V. Thornton	68. S. Stewart Stitt
69. Innes A. Stewart Stitt	70. Henry Walker
71. Harry Nicholls	72. James Powell
73. William Lestocq	74. Frederick H. Buckmaster
75. Herbert William Hodges	76. George Augustus Keen
77. H. Newman Godward	78. Henry Edward Peacock
79. William John C. Nourse	80. Albert Edward George
81. Ellis Vivian Reynolds	82. Paul N. Hasluck

Many of those whose names appear on that list went on to enjoy successful careers in speculative freemasonry (e.g. S.Clifton Bingham and Frank Marquis, who both became Grand Masters in their own countries). Eleven of them eventually became founders of the London Section authorised by Stretton in 1913, and their contribution to the Operatives will be outlined in Chapter 2. Others, however, became influential in promoting the claims of the Operatives by giving talks and writing books to support those claims, and it is proposed to use the remainder of this chapter to provide a thumbnail sketch of each of that particular group because - collectively - they played a vital part in creating the climate of research which ultimately stimulated the growth of this Society. They were: John Yarker, Major A. Gorham, Rev'd S. Stewart Stitt, Arthur Bowes, Robert Bennett Grant, John Gavin Purser, Charles Hope Merz, and Dr. Thomas Carr. Like that of Stretton, it is felt that their names should be known by the members of this Society because although, in the short term, not all of them became Founders of the London Section, they were all men who, in the long term, played an important part in ensuring the success of the Society.

JOHN YARKER: If Stretton can be described as the 'driving force' behind the revival of the two Guild lodges in Leicestershire and the creation of a London Section, then Yarker was unquestionably the most charismatic and internationally well-known of those associated with the early days of the Society, and this is reflected in the list of members quoted earlier in which he is shown first amongst those named. He was born on 17th April 1833 in the village of Swindale, Westmoreland into what was known as a 'good family' which could trace its antecedents to 1399. His family, which had been armigerous for five centuries, were the Yarkers of Leyburn Hall, and he is said to have been the thirteenth in descent from Rheinhold Yarker de Laybourne. Having said that, Yarker's branch of the family left Swindale when he was sixteen and moved to Lancashire, and he eventually settled in a suburb of Manchester known as West Didsbury, which is only mentioned because he wrote 'West Didsbury' on almost everything he published thereafter.

Yarker was initiated into freemasonry at the age of twenty-one in the Lodge of Integrity No. 189 and within three years had joined and become Master of the Lodge of Fidelity No. 633 in nearby Duckinfield. He soon became disillusioned, however, and thereafter was always more enthusiastic about the smaller Orders, resigning from Craft freemasonry entirely in 1862. This is not to say that he lost interest in freemasonry in general and, in a long career, he became a member of many Orders, including:

Knights Templar, under whose banner he was active in reviving and working various lesser-known degrees, such as the Knights of Malta, Red Cross, Rose Croix, and the Royal Arch Knight Templar Priests;

The Ancient and Accepted Rite, in which, despite being in conflict with the Order in England, he received more than twelve 33° Patents from various parts of the world;

The Ancient and Primitive Rite, of which he became the Grand Master in 1902 and, later, Imperial Grand Hierophant 97°;

The Rite of Mizraim, of which he was Sovereign Grand Master from 1871 until his death in 1913.

For his masonic scholarship and literary work he was elected a member of the Masonic Archaeological Institute of London (1862); made Past Senior Grand Warden of the Grand Lodge of Greece (1874); appointed Supreme Grand Master of the Swedenborg Rite (1876); made Honorary Member and Gold Medallist of the Grand Lodge of Roumania (1881); created an

Honorary Grand Master of the Grand Lodge of Cuba (1907); appointed Honorary Grand Master ad vitam of the United Supreme Grand Council of Italy at Firenze, and of the Society Alchemica (1910-12); plus countless other honours. He was also awarded the Star of Merit by the Rajah of Calcutta, and the Constantinian Order of St. George by H.H. Demetrius Rhodancanakis, Hereditary Grand Master and Prince of Rhodes (1874), and received numerous Fellowships and Doctorates.

Throughout all this time he contributed articles to publications such as the *Freemason*, the *Free Mason's Magazine*, the *Free Mason's Chronicle,* the *Kneph* (of which he was publisher and editor from 1881) and to the *Transactions* of the Quatuor Coronati Lodge of Masonic Research No. 2076, starting with *The Unrecognized lodges and degrees of freemasonry before and after 1717* (which appeared in their first volume of Transactions), whilst subsequent papers covered topics such as *Notes in reference to H.Ab, The Old Swalwell Lodge and the Harodim, the Haughfoot Lodge, On Masonic History,* and *Two Ancient Legends concerning the 1st Temple - termed Solomon's Temple.* To put his writings in context, in 1976 one researcher identified at least thirty-five of Yarker's publications in the Library of the United Grand Lodge in London.

By far Yarker's greatest contribution to masonic research, however, was his monumental work *The Arcane Schools* (1909) which took ten years to research and which has been described as "the flower of his devotion to the Craft, and the crown of all his labours...". Chapters IX - XI are of particular relevance to Guild masonry, and it is considered important that, in those chapters, he claimed "It is not supposed that any quarrel occurred at York to separate the Operatives and the Speculatives; the former continued to hold their meetings at High XII, and the latter withdrew to meet in the evening; and their Ritual retained much of the Operative customs not now found in the modern ritual of 1813." Later on he reinforced that claim by pointing out that "In all these years, the old Operative Guilds of Free Masons have continued their work without changing the secrecy of their proceedings. They have their lodges in London, Norfolk, Derbyshire, Holyhead, Leicester, York, Durham, Berwick and elsewhere. Of late years they seem to have become disgusted with the vain pretensions of Modern Speculative Freemasonry and, under authority of the three co-equal GMMs of the South and North, have to some little extent relaxed the secrecy of their proceedings; and though the greater part of their members are utterly averse to anything whatever being made public."

That Yarker was an able scholar is undeniable and although at one time frequently criticised, he has more recently been partially rehabilitated by John Hamill who concluded that "We would be foolish, however, to dismiss his writings out of hand, for amongst the dross are nuggets of pure gold. Were it not for his researches and writing much of the evidence he provides for working the degrees beyond the Craft in the eighteenth and early nineteenth centuries would have remained undiscovered or lost."[11]

Perhaps the last word on Yarker as one of those who greatly assisted Stretton in his cause, should be left to Yarker himself who, in April 1910, when writing about the legacy of the Operatives in the *Co-Mason* magazine, claimed: "I knew of these rites in 1856 or ten years before Bros. Stretton or G.W.Anson knew anything of the matter and I allude to the recent paper of the latter which seems to be an interesting account of an operative initiation at about 14 years of age. At the date just mentioned 1856-7 I knew a Bro.

Eaton of the St. Ninian's Lodge who informed me that he and his fathers had been operative and speculative masons for seven generations."

MAJOR A. GORHAM was a former officer of the Royal Irish Fusiliers and, like Stretton, an office-bearer of the York Division of the Operative Free Masons. He did much to draw attention to the claims of the Operatives by writing papers and giving talks to research groups such as the Somerset Masters' Lodge No. 3746, but particularly deserves to be remembered for two claims, both of which were made in one of his lectures published in 1919. The first was that "We should all be interested in and pride ourselves on our descent from ancient Operative masonry, whose monuments are to be found throughout the world", and the second was that "There should be no mistake about the status of Operative Masonry, which was a Religion and a Trade combined."[12]

Other publications by Major Gorham include a book on *Indian Masons' Marks of the Moghul Dynasty*; papers on *Observations on some Points & Sytmbolism in ritual* (1929) and *Secrets of the Ancient Architects* (1932) both published in the *Transactions* of the Masonic Study Society; and *The Kennet and Avon Canal and its Marks* (1920) published by the Somerset Masters Lodge No. 3746.

REV'D SAMUEL STEWART STITT was the vicar of Streatham and Little Thetford, near Ely, Cambridgeshire, and believed, just as fervently as Major Gorham, that Operative free masonry was a "Religion and a Trade combined" and wrote a paper to that effect published in *The Aldershot Army and Navy Lodge Journal* for October 1912 under the title "What is the Debt Speculative Freemasonry owes to the Operative Society?" He followed that up with another entitled "The Operative Freemasons" which appeared in the same publication in January 1913 in which he explained the use of the distinctive rods carried by the three Master Masons and the layout of an Operative's lodge. So enthusiastic was he concerning the Operatives that he was unsuccessfully urged by Stretton to consider forming a Guild lodge in East Anglia and he proposed both of his sons for membership of the Mount Bardon Lodge, i.e. Innes D'Auvergn Stewart Stitt who - like the stonemasons of old - was indentured at the age of fourteen, and George Marquis Stewart Stitt, who later became an officer in the army but was killed in action during the 1st World War.

ARTHUR BOWES was an engineer resident in Newton-le-Willows, Lancashire, and a regular contributor to publications such as *The Freemason* (e.g. 'Freemasonry before 1717', and 'The Teachings of Pythagoras') and contributed several papers to the Leicester Lodge of Research No. 2429 on topics such as Modern Masons' Marks (1906), Masonic Secrets of the Pyramids (1910), The 3-4-5 Triangle (1911), and The Broached Thurnal (1912).

That he was an avid supporter of Stretton and Yarker as far as their claims were concerned, is evident from a letter he wrote to *The Freemason* on 1st September 1909 in which he stated "Personally I am more concerned with the truths contained in the revelations of Gild (sic) teaching which have recently been made; if the message is a helpful and enlightening one I can dispense with the official stamp on the paper which carries it. When I find the statements of Gild Masons verified by innumerable details in Lodge and Chapter...by anomalies in our present working...by the measurements of buildings which date back to many hundreds years in Europe and many thousand years in Egypt...etc. etc...I am compelled to recognise the value of Gild teaching. If entirely unsupported by other evidence I look upon it with respect and am anxious to investigate it to the utmost."

ROBERT BENNETT GRANT was Superintendent of the Bardon Hill Quarries for thirty-two years and, like Stretton, contributed articles concerning the Operatives to *The Co-Mason* magazine which did so much at a national level to draw attention to the claims of the Operatives. Especially one (*The Arms of the Worshipful Society of Free Masons*) of April 1910 concerning a Charter given by Bishop Morton in the 17th Century to the Worshipful Society of Free Masons, Rough Masons, Wallers, Slaters, Paviors, Plaisterers and Bricklayers of Durham, which title the Society of 1913 adopted as its own. He also contributed articles to local newspapers, such as the *Coalville Times* and the *Melton Mowbray Times*.

JOHN GAVIN PURSER was an Irish freemason living at Howth, near Dublin, Ireland, whose enthusiasm for operative free masonry was such that, according to Philip Crossle, writing from Freemasons' Hall, Dublin, after Purser's death in 1935, "...his whole heart and sympathy was given to the objects of the Operative Masons". This was clearly recognised by Stretton because, at a meetings of the two Leicester Guild lodges on 3rd April 1915 it was "Resolved that the Brethren who have duly signed and sealed the Oath of Nimrod...are hereby Elected Members of Lodges 110 and 91 which are established at Bardon Hill, Leicester, England, by virtue of a Charter granted to masons by King Athelstan AD 926 and by virtue of 2 other Charters granted by the York Division AD 1761 and 1831. Resolved that the application of the aforesaid brethren now residing in or near the City of Dublin, Ireland, be granted and authority given to open, form, consecrate and erect at Dublin a lodge of Free Masons,

Rough Masons, Wallers, Slaters, Paviors, Plaisterers and Bricklayers to be known by the name of the Clement Edwin Stretton Lodge of Research on the Roll of the York Division of this Worshipful Society.   Resolved that Brother John G. Purser be appointed the Consecrating Officer and First Master Mason, Bro. Arthur E. Porte be second Master Mason and Bro. Hy. L. Bourke be third Master Mason. And you the said Three Master Masons of Lodge 110 Dublin Section are further required as soon as conveniently may be to send to us an account in writing of what shall be done by virtue of those present. Given under our Hands and Seal in open Assembly this 3rd day of April 1915.   By command of the Master Masons of the "York Division", Mount Bardon Lodge No. 110 and 91 Leicester.   Robert B. Grant 1st Master Mason, W.G.A.Bailey 2nd Master Mason, and Frank T. Bellward 3rd Master Mason."

Nothing resulted from that initiative, but that is hardly surprising given that, by that time, the 1st World War was in progress, and Ireland was experiencing its own internal problems which resulted in the famous Proclamation of 1916 and, eventually, the creation of the Republic of Ireland. In short, despite the best of intentions on the part of Stretton (who died in 1915) and Purser, they were hardly the most propitious of times in which to attempt to form an English masonic lodge in Ireland.

DR. CHARLES HOPE MERZ was born at Oxford, Ohio on 7th November 1861 and was educated at Miami University, Oxford and Western Reserve University, Cleveland, graduating in medicine in 1885. Thereafter he practiced that profession in Sandusky, Ohio , but still found time to be heavily involved in freemasonry, attaining the chair as Master of Science Lodge No. 50, and becoming a member of several other Orders such as the

Royal Arch, Royal and Select Masters, Knights Templar, an Erie Commandery, and the Scottish Rite in which he attained the 32º. He is, probably best remembered for having served twenty-eight years as the editor of the Sandusky Masonic Bulletin. He is mentioned in William R. Denslow's book *10,000 Famous Freemasons* and is also remembered as the author of several books, including *The House of Solomon, When Temples were Inns,* and, very importantly, *Guild Masonry in the Making* (Light Publishing Co.) 1918. Interestingly, in the front of the last named book, Merz reproduced a letter from Stretton dated 5th October 1912, which reads: "At a meeting of the Master Masons of the York Division held at York this day, Charles H. Merz, Master Mason, VIIº was appointed as Special Representative of this Society in America. By Order of the Master Masons. Clement E. Stretton, Secretary."

The author of this book has since obtained a photocopy of a letter subsequently written and signed by Merz which reads: "To Whom it may concern. As Special Representative and Secretary of the above named Worshipful Society in America, a commission granted to me by order of the Masters on October 5th, 1912, I hereby authorize the Masonic Brethren in Monroe, S.C., U.S.A. to organize and maintain a branch of that Society in the said city of Monroe, N.C.(sic) (Signed) Charles H. Merz, M.D., Sandusky, Ohio, VIIº Y Jan 2, 1933." By then, unfortunately, whatever impetus might have existed twenty years earlier had evaporated, and, despite the involvement of such eminent American masons as J.Raymond Shute and William Moseley Brown, his belated initiative (like that or Stitt in East Anglia and Purser in Ireland) came to nothing, and the freemasons of America had to wait another seventy-five years for their first Assemblage on American soil. His writings, however, unquestionably sustained the case for the Operatives throughout the U.S.A..

DR. THOMAS CARR was a highly respected member of the two operative lodges at Bardon Hill, of whom Dr. Merz wrote "Brother Dr. Thomas Carr is a distinguished Mason of Blackpool. He is a man of great learning and ability and the author of a number of valuable Masonic works. It is to Dr. Carr that the public is indebted for the principle facts concerning the Operative Ritual."[13]

He was both a medical doctor and a barrister, a Past Master of Fylde Lodge No. 2758, a member of the Leicester Lodge of Research, and a Past Grand Warden of the Province of Lancashire, but is now best remembered for two things. Firstly, for having been given permission by working Guild operative masons to perpetuate details of their history, organisation and rituals in a book entitled *The ritual of the Operative Free Masons*, published in 1911, and giving a talk on that subject to the Manchester Association for Masonic Research later that year. And, secondly, after it had been decided to form a London Section in 1913 to preserve and perpetuate the ceremonies of the moribund Guild, it was he who was authorised by Stretton to open that Section and install Colonel Henry Walker as its 1st Master Mason.

As was explained in the Introduction, the London Section (now known as Channel Row Assemblage) has remained in existence ever since, and it is to its formation in May 1913, and the events of the Society's first fifty years, that we can now turn our attention.

REFERENCES

1. Carr, H. '600 Years of Craft Masonry' in *Ars Quatuor Coronatorum* Vol. 81, 1968, pp. 153-180

2. Haywood, H.L."Freemasonry and the Guild System' in *The Builder* magazine, Vo. IX, 1923

3. Jones, B.E. *Freemasonry's debt to the Guilds*, 1960

4. Hughan, W.J. *The Old Charges* (1872) p.8

5. Duffell, S. 'Clement E. Stretton' in the *Journal of the Railway & Canal Historical Society* Vol.35, Part 3, November 2005

6. Stretton, C.E. 'Guild Masonry' in the *Transactions* of the Leicester Lodge of Research No. 2429 for 1910

7. Seal-Coon, F.W. 'An old-time Operative Midsummer Ceremony' in *Ars Quatuor Coronatorum* Vol.105 pp161-171

8. Carr, T. *The ritual of the Operative Free Masons* (Tyler Publishing) 1911, p.17

9. Cryer, N.B. *The Arch and the Rainbow* (Lewis Masonic) 1996, p.26

10. Dat, B. 'The Operative Masonry of Stretton: Restoration or Contrivance?' in *Renaissance Traditionelle* Issue No. 118-119 April - July 1999

11. Hamill, J. 'John Yarker: Masonic Charlatan?' in *Ars Quatuor Coronatorum* Vol.109, 1996, p.198

12. Gorham, A. 'Operative Masonry' in the *Transactions* of the Somerset Masters Lodge No. 3746, 1919, p.31

13 Merz, C.H. *Guild Masonry in the Making* (Light Publishing) 1918, p.17

CHAPTER 2

The first fifty years (1913-1963)

There was nothing spectacular about the first fifty years of the Operatives and, if it is necessary to identify something impressive or even mildly surprising concerning that period, the only thing that comes to mind is that, at the end of it, the Society was still in existence at all! That having been said, and whether surprising or not, there were some events which have to be placed on record if only to ensure the completeness of this record and they include: The 'revival' of the London Section; the founding of a Court of Assistants; the support given by two other masonic organisations; the constituting of three more Assemblages; and the effect on freemasonry of the end of the 2nd World War. That being so, it is proposed to describe them under those sub-headings.

The 'revival' of the London Section

On 21st May eleven members of Mount Bardon Lodge attended a meeting at the Bijou Theatre in Bedford Street, London, W.C., which is a side-street leading from the Strand to Covent Garden. The Bijou Theatre occupied a large upstairs room in No. 3, one end of which had been fitted with a stage.

No. 3 Bedford Street today

It is now mostly remembered for its association with the Ben Greet Academy of Acting and, in reality, was more of a rehearsal studio than a commercial theatre. Conveniently, on the day of the meeting, it was owned (or leased) by Paul N. Hasluck, who was one of the eleven founders. A list of those attending that meeting is reproduced below, the number after each name indicating the position of that person on the list of members of Mount Bardon Lodge shown on pages 15-16:

1   W. Bro. Dr. Thomas Carr (No. 23)

2   Colonel Henry Walker (No. 70)

3   Harry Nicholls (No. 71)

4   James Powell (No. 72)

5   Paul N. Hasluck (No. 82)

6   Ellis Vivian Reynolds (No. 81)

7   Major A. Gorham (No. 35)

8   Frederick Henry Buckmaster ((No. 74)

9   W. J. Chichele Nourse (No. 79)

10   H. Newman Godward (No. 77)

11   Albert Edward George (No. 80)

Even though one of their number owned the building, there was probably more than financial expediency involved in their choice of the theatre as a meeting place because, apart from their interest in ancient free masonry (which is presumably what had attracted them to an operative lodge in the first place) most were professionally involved in the theatre, so they would have been familiar with that theatre and known that it was a suitable venue for their purposes. Freemasonry and theatres, it should be explained, have enjoyed a long association with the Covent Garden area, as described by David Peabody in *Freemasonry Today*[1] and J.W.Reddyhoff in AQC Vol.105[2]. Additionally, most of them were members of at least one of those London lodges which cater for the masonic needs of actors, such as the Drury Lane Lodge (which still meets in the Theatre Royal, near to the Bijou Theatre), the Lodge of Asaph, the Green Room Lodge, and the Dramatic Mark and Royal Ark Mariner Lodges, so they would probably have felt more 'at home' in a theatre. Given those circumstances it is tempting to terminate any further discussion of their backgrounds by simply pointing to the obvious, which is that they were all freemasons and mostly actors, and leaving it at that. The truth, however, is that they were all much more than that, and not to explain their backgrounds would be to do them, and the reader, a disservice.

For example, the contribution of Dr. Carr and Major Gorham to this Society, has already been mentioned on pages 21-26; but Colonel Henry Walker's background is equally important because he was a distinguished soldier and a Grand Officer, well known in London masonic circles who, at one point in his masonic career, famously presided at a dinner held in the Holborn Restaurant, attended by the Prince of Wales, the Duke of Connaught, the Lord Chancellor, the Earl of Londesborough, Sir Henry Irving, and other notable masonic personages of the period. He was a member of the Drury Lane Lodge No. 2127 and so was accustomed to rubbing-shoulders with the likes of Field Marshal Lord Kitchener and Captain Robert Falcon Scott (i.e. Scott of the Antartic) who were members of that prestigious lodge, as demonstrated by a letter concerning Kitchener sent to Colonel Walker as WM of Drury Lane Lodge, reproduced in *The Freemason* for 13th April

1912. Two of the other Founders (Harry Nicholls and James Powell) were also members of Drury Lane Lodge, and Harry Nicholls was not only a Grand Officer of Craft masonry but a playright and actor of repute, of whom there are six portraits in the National Portrait Gallery. He is also referred to in Andrew Prescott's paper on *Brother Irving: Sir Henry Irving and Freemasonry* (2011). Ellis Vivian Reynolds was equally as famous as a stage actor but, in addition, was in the process of building a second career in the new medium of film. Frederick H. Buckmaster is now remembered as the author of the official history of the Royal Order of Scotland and a variety of other masonic attainments and, after his death, was described by Dudley Wright as "an ardent student of Masonry in all its branches, and one who was a thorough exemplification of what a mason should be in practice as well as in idealism"[3]. Finally, Paul Hasluck was a successful author who wrote many books on practical subjects (e.g. Wood Working, Cabinetwork & Joinery, Bamboo Work, How to write Signs and Posters, etc.) and, as already mentioned, he was the owner (or lessee) of the Bijou Theatre. To summarise, they were all men of attainment and ability, and well suited to their role as founders of an Operative lodge designed to perpetuate ancient Guild practices.

In retrospect, they appear to have had two reasons for attending the meeting at the Bijou Theatre, the most obvious of which was to create (or 'revive') a London Section of their operative lodge in Leicestershire, so that they could continue their research into the ritual, procedures and language of the ancient Guild masons without the inconvenience and cost of travelling to and from Leicester. But a second reason, which would inevitably result from the first, was to re-constitute the former Westminster

Division which, it will be remembered, was one of the eight Guild Divisions originally created in 1677. A possible indication of the strength of their feeling towards that Division is provided by the first seal of the Society, displayed on the back cover of this book, which emphasises the Westminster connection.

The notice convening the meeting read as follows: "The next Regular Meeting of the London Section will be held under the joint sanction of Lodge 'Leicester' No.91 and Lodge 'Mount Bardon' No. 110 at 5.15 p.m. on Wednesday 21st May 1913, at the Bijou Theatre (Hasluck's Academy), Bedford House, 3 Bedford Street, Strand, W.C. (Signed) Clement E. Stretton, VII°, Secretary, York Division". (N.B. The use of the word 'next' in this connection is important because it provides the only justification for considering the creation of a London Section a 'revival' as distinct from a constitution or re-constitution, and it can only be assumed that Stretton's reason for referring to it in that way was his belief (or assumption) that, if there had once been a Westminster Division then, ipso facto, there must - at some time - have been a London lodge of operative masons within that Division. Ergo (though requiring a certain amount of creative imagination) the meeting of 21st May 1913 might legitimately be described as their 'next' meeting rather than their 'first'. Alternatively, and more plausibly, he might simply have used the word 'next' in order to invest the new London Section with an aura of antiquity it would not otherwise enjoy. One hundred years after the event, it is unlikely that we will ever know which explanation is nearer the truth.)

According to the Rev'd R.R.à-Ababrelton[4], W.Bro. Carr duly carried out the duties of Enthroning Officer and began by reading the following letter from Stretton, authorising the meeting: "Dear Sirs and Brothers, I am instructed to inform you that the Masters of

Lodges 91 and 110 have deputed Brother Thomas Carr, Third Master Mason of Lodge 91, to attend at London on 21st May, to open a Master Masons' Lodge in the VIIth degree. To enthrone the three Master Masons designate of the London Section. To carry out all other work in accordance with the ancient usages and established customs as Enthroned Master Masons have done in all ages. By Order of the Masters, Clement E. Stretton, Secretary".

He then appointed Colonel Henry Walker, Harry Nicholls and James Powell 1st, 2nd and 3rd Master Masons respectively; Ellis Vivian Reynolds and Major A. Gorham were appointed Deputies Jachin and Boaz; and Paul Hasluck was appointed Deputy Master Mason. Finally, W.Bro. Carr delivered a lecture on 'The Worshipful Society of Freemasons, Rough Masons, Wallers, Slaters, Paviors, Plaisterers and Bricklayers' and the meeting was brought to an end.

In this way, a London Section of the two Leicestershire Guild lodges was 'revived', the former Westminster Division was re-constituted, and the first steps were taken in the life of the Society which has since become known as 'The Operatives'.

The London Section seems to have met on a monthly basis thereafter, for the first few years at the Bijou Theatre, then at Anderton's Hotel, Fleet Street, London, E.C. but, from the early 1920's until September 1972, at 10 Duke Street, St. James. Because of rising costs they then moved to the National Liberal Club near Charing Cross. Unfortunately, all MInutes of those meetings have long since disappeared, although a few details were preserved by the Rev'd à-Ababrelton for his *Operative Review of 1941*, and by J.D.Bing VII°, Grand Librarian at Mark Masons' Hall, for a paper published in the *Transactions* of the Manchester Association for Masonic Research in 1975[5]. As a result, from *The Operative Review* it is now known that on 4th November 1914 a letter was read from Stretton notifying the members that he had been appointed General Secretary of the Worshipful Society of Operative Freemasons, whilst from the lecture given by Bro. Bing it is known that in March 1915 Bro. F.H.Buckmaster reported the death of Stretton on 20th February, 1915.

Fortunately, Bing also recorded the following resolution passed by the London Section on 14th April, 1915 as a consequence of Stretton's death: "We the three Master Masons of the London Section of Lodges 91 and 110 of the Worshipful Society of Free Masons, Rough Masons, Wallers, Slaters, Paviors, Plaisterers and Bricklayers, formed in 1913 under the authority of York Division No. 8, having learnt with great sorrow of the death of our Worshipful Brother Clement E. Stretton, Secretary of the York Division No. 8 and knowing that it was his wish that we should revive The Westminster Division No. 2 and being well satisfied that the Westminster Division has ceased to exist and being anxious to continue our research work as to Free Masonry prior to 1717 and having the approval of all the Brethren of the London Section and the consent of Lodges Leicester and Mount Bardon, hereby constitute our London Section 'The Channel Row Assemblage' of the Worshipfiul Society of Free Masons, Rough Masons, Wallers, Slaters, Paviors, Plaisterers and Bricklayers, Westminster Division, so called after the Operative Lodge which held its meetings prior to 1717 at The Rummer and Grapes Inn in Channel Row (afterwards altered to Cannon Row), Westminster which was one of the four old Operative Lodges which formed the Grand Lodge of England in 1717." (N.B. Channel Row was a small road close to the point where the River Tyburn joined the Thames near Westminster Bridge and, although all four of the lodges which came together to create the Premier Grand Lodge are known to have been 'operative' in origin, that which met at the Rummer and Grapes Inn, and later became known as the Horn Tavern was, ironically, the least operative of all, many of its members being drawn from men who spent their lives in and around the Palace of Westminster. Interestingly, Dr. John Theophilus Desaguiler, who became Grand Master of of the Premier Grand Lodge in 1719, lived in Channel Row for more than twenty-five years.[6])

The founding of a Court of Assistants

One of the first steps taken by the London Section was to vest responsibility for its administration in a Court of Assistants and, so unusual was this a decision, that it seems to have intrigued virtually all those interested in the early days of this Society ever since. A Court of Assistants, it should be explained, is an administrative body the most common use for which is to govern a 'Trade' association and, although frequently adopted by Livery Companies (e.g. The Worshipful Company of Clockmakers since 1631, and the Worshipful Company of Engineers today), apart from Channel Row Assemblage, they are unknown to modern freemasonry.

Confusingly, there are two explanations for this conundrum, both of which are plausible. The first is that in opting to be administered by a Court of Assistants they were reflecting a decision taken by the London Company of Masons in 1677 when that body was incorporated by Charter from the Crown and control was vested in a Master, two wardens and twenty-four or more Assistants, who were appointed for life.

The second explanation lies in the military background of one of the London Section's founders (Colonel Henry Walker) because it has recently been learned that the Honourable Artillery Company of London, although recognised to be the oldest unit within the British army, is similarly, administered by a Court of Assistants, which has governed the civil and financial affairs of that Company since 1633. The explanation for this strange phenomenon, it seems, lies in the fact that, as well as being a military unit the Honourable Artillery Company also functions as a Livery Company. Colonel Walker was closely associated with that Company and, more importantly, was the 1st Master Mason of the revived London Section so, for him, creating a Court of Assistants to administer the London Section was an obvious thing to do. In short, he did it because, as a member of the Honourable Artillery Company and a Liveryman, that was how be thought any organization, masonic or otherwise, ought to be administered.

Which of these explanations is the more apposite is now irrelevant because its period of influence lasted only eighteen years but, for a time (i.e immediately following the death of Stretton) it became important as the governing body of the London Section, and so might legitimately be regarded as the precursor of Grand Assemblage. Its existence deserves to be acknowledged for that reason alone, although some of its decisions are equally worthy of mention. For instance: It was the Court of Assistants, which first recommended that the periods of office of the three Master Masons should be five years (1st MM), three years (2nd MM), and one year (3rd MM) respectively, which is still the position today as far as the three Grand Master Masons are concerned. Also that the Ancient Drama, involving a re-enactment of the murder of Hiram Abiff, should be performed annually in October which, again, is still the position today although, for reasons of administrative convenience, the date has recently been brought forward to late-September.

Another important decision of the Court of Assistants, the wording of which reflects the Society's Livery associations, was that: "In future the composition of the Court be the three Master Masons, Clerk, Treasurer, and the last joined member ex officio and four elected members; the Court being ruled by the 1st Master Mason, the 2nd and 3rd Master Masons and last joined member being first, second and Renter Wardens respectfully." (N.B. Renter Wardens, like Courts of Assistants, are unknown in modern freemasonry but, In Livery Companies, a Renter Warden's duties include collecting rents and making payments on behalf of a Company, in conjunction with its Treasurer.)

By far its most important recommendation, however, was that agreed on 22nd July 1931 when the Court of Assistants (which invariably met at the offices of H.Newman Godward, its Treasurer, at 51 Victoria Street, London, W.1) resolved that Channel Row Assemblage should accept the following recommendation: "That we the Channel Row Assemblage of the Westminster Division of the Worshipful Society of Free Masons, Rough Masons, Wallers, Slaters, Paviors, Plaisterers and Bricklayers, being a lodge of Operative Free Masons, do by these presents constitute and form into a Grand Assembly of Operative Free Masons our Brothers as follows:

Henry T. Cart de la Fontaine, VII°
Frederick Conkling Van Duzer, VII°
Dudley P. Hutchings, VII°
Bernard Henry Springett, VII°
Right Hon Sir Frederick Pollock, Bart.K.C.,LL.D.,D.C.L., VII°

Percy Plowman, VII°

George Sherrington Collins, VII°

Col. F.M.Rickard, R.A., VII°

Brig.-Gen.W.H.Sitwell, D.S.O., VII°

Major A. Gorham, VII°

Sir A.A.Brooke-Pechell, Bart., VII°

M.J.Beever Anderson, VII°

P.W.Morehen, VII°

Langford H.MacKelcken, VII°

G.E.W.Bridge, VII°

George B.Cotton, VII°

George Russell, VII°

Thomas F. Jolly, VII°

John Edward Whitty, VII°

John Lawrance

Arthur Skinner

with jurisdiction over all Lodges of Operative Free Masons in that portion of England and Wales south of the Rivers Humber, Trent, Dane, Weaver and Mersey, denominated the Westminster Division of the Worshipful Society, with powers to make Rules and Regulations for the governance of the Division and all such Lodges and for the Constitution and governance of new Lodges of Operative Free Masons within the Division." That recommendation was duly accepted by the Assemblage but its area of jurisdiction has since been extended indefinitely.

The Court's final meeting was on 12th October 1931, on which occasion it was necessary to elect a new 1st Master Mason, the incumbent (Samuel Blaze Wilkinson) having died during the intervening period. At that meeting it was also agreed to defer the dissolution of the Court of Assistants until a later date although, in the event, that was its last meeting, responsibility for the administration of the Assemblage thereafter devolving upon the newly formed Grand Assemblage, which came into existence with effect from 19th October 1931.

The support given by two other masonic organisations

During the first fifty years of the Society's existence, support for the claims of the Stretton and his colleagues notably came from two other masonic organizations; i.e. the Co-Masons (a mixed society of male and female freemasons) and the Masonic Study Society (a research society founded in 1921). The nature of that support, and the circumstances under which it was given, are as follows.

As far as the Co-Masons are concerned, it has already been explained that one of Stretton's strategies for promoting the claims of the Operatives was to encourage his supporters to submit letters and articles concerning the Guild to local newspapers and masonic publications, such as *The Co-Mason,* a quarterly magazine edited and published by J.A.Bothwell-Gosse. Although he was not aware of it at that time, J.A.Bothwell-Gosse was, in fact, M.Ill.Bro. J.Aimee Bothwell-Gosse, a distinguished lady-mason, whose "life was largely devoted to Freemasonry, first in the Co-Masonic Movement and from 1925 onwards as Founding Head of The Order of Ancient Free and Accepted Masonry for Men and Women". Given those circumstances, nearly a century later, it seems curious that correspondence from the Society was for such a long time addressed to Bro. J.A.Bothwell-Gosse Esq. and invariably began with the words 'Dear Sir'. Having said that, however, it needs to be remembered that, at that time, the Suffragette Movement was still in its infancy, and ladies were obliged to wait another twenty years before they were enfranchised on the same terms as men. It is hardly surprising, therefore, that anyone receiving correspondence from someone describing themselves as a 'Brother' should assume that the writer was male, In which connection, it is possibly worth adding that, even today, some lady-masons still choose to address their colleagues as 'Brother', on a basis that, whether male or female, they are all members of the 'Brotherhood of Freemasonry'.

That having been explained, and before concluding this sub-section, it is considered appropriate at this point to provide a few further details concerning Miss Bothwell-Gosse, not because she was such a remarkable lady, but because she was a staunch advocate and friend of the Operatives and her contribution to this Society in its early years deserves to be placed on record.

She was initiated into co-masonry in 1904, in the Lodge Human Duty No. 6 and eventually went on to form five Craft lodges, one Mark lodge, a Royal Arch Chapter, and the first Supreme Council of the Ancient and Accepted Rite in women's freemasonry. She was a successful teacher, an accomplished pianist, a Theosophist, and the author of numerous books, including the *Knights Templar* (1912), *The Civilization of the Ancient Egyptians* (1915), *The Magic of the Pyramids and the Mystery of the Sphinx* (1915), *The Rose Immortal* (1916), *A short sketch of the Ancient and Accepted Scottish Rite* (1926), and *The Lily of Light* (1935). More importantly as far as this Society is concerned, she was so impressed by the claims of Stretton and Yarker that, from about 1908 onwards, she proved an invaluable ally by not only publishing articles in the *Co-Mason* (a magazine which she edited and published herself) concerning the Operatives but wrote articles of her own in support of those claims, such as her papers on *Astronomy and Masonry* and *The Master Masons'*

Square Talisman. Eventually she proved to be the best of all possible allies by joining the Operatives herself, which she did by accepting invitations to become a member of both Mount Bardon Lodge No. 110 and Leicester Lodge No. 91, and it speaks volumes for the support she had given the Operatives that when it finally dawned on the members of those lodges that their long-time correspondent was a lady-mason, they welcomed her anyway, and she eventually attained the VII° degree and the status of a Grand Master Mason, which title she used for the remainder of her life. In fact, in her Obituary (published in *The Speculative* Mason) she was referred to as "M.Ill. Bro.J.Aimee Bothwell-Goose, 33°, Grand Master VII° of the Guild of Operative Freemasons, Founder and Most Puissant Sovereign Grand Commander 1925-50 of the Order of Ancient Free and Accepted Masonry for Men and Women, Founder and Editor of this Magazine 1909-1948"[7].

It was certainly fortunate for the Society that she attained that rank because, on 22nd April 1931, Bernard Springett found it necessary to write the following revealing letter to her. "Dear Miss Bothwell-Gosse, Our Channel Row Assemblage of Operative Masons is now so large and includes so many keen masons that there is a general desire to see the higher degrees working in full, instead of merely communicated, which was all Sir John Cockburn thought necessary, a wise precaution as he did not know the Ritual. I know that as you are the sole survivor as far as I know of the Mount Bardon Lodge you hold the key to these Rituals. Knowing also your kindlly disposition of which I have had such full experience I venture to ask you to come to the rescue if you can and will. Of course a certain amount of valuable information was given in back issues of the *Co-Mason* but can you disclose with due precautions the "Secrets" which are necessary? By doing so you would earn the everlasting gratitude of many worthy Operatives and especially of Yours very sincerely, B.H.Springett". (N.B. Springett, in fact, was wrong in supposing Miss Bothwell-Goose to be the only surviving member of Mount Bardon Lodge, both Robert Bennet Grant and the Rev'd. S. Stewart Stitt still being alive at that time. In fact Grant was still attending to queries concerning Mount Bardon Lodge as late as 20th March 1934, and the Society has in its archives a letter written by Grant on that date on Mount Bardon Lodge stationery. He died on 19th December 1938, on which date he was 87. Nor had the Rev. S. Stewart Stitt forgotten his involvement with Mount Bardon Lodge for, on 4th May 1938, he returned the Indenture form of his son George Marquis Stitt (killed in action in 1918) to the Grand Clerk. Rev. Stitt died on 12th May 1939.)

After her death in 1954, Miss Bothwell-Gosse's involvement with the Operatives was continued by her successor as editor of *The Speculative Mason*, M.Ill.Bro. Marjorie Cecily Debenham, Grand Master *ad vitam* of the Order of Ancient Free and Accepted Masonry for Men and Women, who was every bit as remarkable a lady as Miss Bothwell-Gosse. She was a member of the famous department-store family, a multi-linguist, and a Buddhist. And not only did she continue to reprint and publish the papers of Stretton, Yarker et al but published her own papers in explanation of those ideas, such as those of 1951 concerning *Ancient Guild Masonry* and *The Death Drama*. More importantly, it was she who ensured the preservation of vast quantities of correspondence between Stretton and Yarker, and between Stretton and Miss Bothwell-Gosse, and went on (in conjunction with Charlotte Elizabeth Jones) to re-invigorate interest in those ideas by co-operating with F.W.Seal-Coon, a Past Master of Quatuor Coronati

Lodge No. 2076, in the preparation of his paper on *An Old-Time 'Operative' Midsummer Ceremony* published in AQC Volume 105 (1992). That paper chiefly concerns the Co-Masons but, at the same time, reflects much that was written about by Stretton and his colleagues concerning Guild free masonry.

M.Ill.Bros. Bothwell-Gosse and Majorie Debenham were unquestionably good friends of the Operatives and, it might be argued, had it not been for them, the Operatives might never have enjoyed the early success that they did. Interestingly, together with Charlotte Jones, they were themselves the subject of a book (*We three or three such as we*) in the Introduction to which it is explained that "This book captures moments in the life of three women Freemasons over a period of 150 years: Aimee Bothwell-Gosse, Majorie C.Debenham and Charlotte Jones. They were honoured with the 33rd Degree, the highest degree of the Ancient and Accepted Scottish Rite, for their lifelong dedication. Yet their stories are mostly unknown"[8]. By highlighting their contribution to Operative free masonry in *this* book it is hoped that this Society has, in a small way, gone some way towards reversing that trend and, to the members of this Society at least, they will not be 'unknown' in the future.

Having, therefore, explained the support given by the Co-Masons, let us now turn our attention to the assistance provided by another masonic organization, the Masonic Study Society, a society formed in 1921 which, from the outset, supported - and was supported by - the Operatives. In fact, it has been suggested that, as a society, it only came into existence as a result of the disappointment felt by some of the early Operatives who would have preferred their Assemblage to have been a research lodge rather than a lodge dedicated to working the ceremonies of their

Guild predecessors. Having failed in that respect, they appear to have founded the Masonic Study Society as a sort of after-thought to assuage their appetite for research. As a result, from the outset, the two societies had numerous members in common and, to name only the most well-known, they included:

The Hon. Sir JOHN ALEXANDER COCKBURN who was born in Berwickshire and educated at Highgate School and King's College, London. In 1875 he emigrated to Australia where he eventually became the Minister for Education, Prime Minister and the Deputy Grand Master for South Australia. On returning to this country, he joined the Operatives on 3rd November 1915 and in 1918 became the 1st Master Mason of Channel Row Assemblage, an office he held until his death in 1929. As far as the Masonic Study Society is concerned, he was the founding Vice-President in 1921 and delivered many lectures on an operative theme which are now preserved in the *Transactions* of that Society for 1921,1922,1923, 1925 and 1927. His paper *Operative and Ancient Freemasonry* which explains many of the 'secrets' of Operative Free Masonry, is still available on Wikipedia, as is his Obituary, published in the British Medical Journal for 1929.

JOHN SEBASTIAN MARLOW WARD spent time in the army and as a customs officer. He also enjoyed the distinction of being created a Bishop three times over, and was the owner of the Abbey Folk Park in Barnet. He wrote many books on masonic themes, not least of which were his Handbooks for an Entered Apprentice, Fellow of the Craft, and Master Mason, all of which have Introductions by Sir John Cockburn. As far as the Masonic Study Society is concerned, he was its first Secretary-General, a member of its Council and of its Board of Editors. He became a member of the Operatives on 20th December 1920 and is now best remembered for having recovered the notebooks of John Yarker containing details of the seven degrees worked by this Society. In short, it is J.S.M.Ward that the Society has to thank for most of its ritual.

ARTHUR EDWARD WAITE was a prolific author whose writings are redolent with Operative references. For instance, his reference to the Building Guilds in his New Encyclopedia of Freemasonry Vol.1 in which (on page 81) he states: "As Emblematical Freemasonry is the Craft of Building moralised, it follows that - intellectually at least - our figurative and speculative art has arisen out of the Operative." He joined Channel Row Assemblage on 12th January 1916, and was the founding Deputy Vice-President of the Masonic Study Society in 1921.

HENRY T. CART DE LAFONTAINE was the Prestonian Lecturer for 1930 when his topic was "The Seven Liberal Arts and Sciences" which is a subject of major importance to the Operatives. He was Master of Quatuor Coronati Lodge No. 2076 for 1929-30, and wrote several papers published in their Transactions. He served the Masonic Study Society as its first Orator and was a member of its Council and of its Board of Editors. As far as the Operatives are concerned, he attained the VII° and was the 2nd Master Mason of Channel Row Assemblage for 1930 and 1931.

BERNARD HENRY SPRINGETT was the author of several books on masonic topics, not least of which is his book on the Mark Degree. As far as the Operatives are concerned, one of his most important publications was a paper which appeared in *The Builder* (a publication of the National Masonic Research Society of the USA) in 1925, entitled: *The Society of operative Stone Masons; its links with Operative and Speculative Masonry of the* *present day.* He has, of course, already been mentioned in this Chapter, having written to Bro. Aimee Bothwell-Gosse in 1931 seeking the secrets of the higher degrees. As an Operative free mason he attained the VII°. In the Masonic Study Society he was a member of its Senate and one of its Board of Editors.

Rt.Hon.Sir FREDERICK POLLOCK, Bart.,K.C.,LL.D., D.C.L. was an internationally recognised authority on Jurisprudence, with Honorary Doctorates from the Universities of Paris, Cambridge, Edinburgh, Dublin, Harvard, Columbia and Oslo. As far as the Masonic Study Society is concerned, he was a member of its Council and of its Senate and gave lectures on "Archaic Element in Craft Ritual " and "Greater Lights in the 18th Century, with some sidelights on early working". In the Operatives he attained the VII° and was the 3rd Master Mason of Channel Row Assemblage in 1922.

There were many others, such as: Samuel Blaze Wilkinson, who was a member of the Senate of the Masonic Study Society, and one of the Master Masons of Channel Row Assemlage from 1924 until 1930; Dudley P.Hutchings, who was a member of the Masonic Study Society's Senate and succeeded Samuel Blaze Wilkinson as the 1st Master Mason of Channel Row Assemblage in 1931; Herbert William Hodges, who was the founding Treasurer-General of the Masonic Study Society and Clerk of Channel Row Assemblage ; and Langford H.MacKelchen, who was a member of the Masonic Study Society's Senate and became 3rd Grand Master Master Mason of the Operatives in 1933.

As explained, there were undoubtedly others who were members of both societies, and that remains the position to the present day. To avoid becoming repetitious, however, it is hoped that the point has already been made which is that,   had the

Masonic Study Society not come into existence soon after Channel Row Assemblage and subsequently helped to sustain and dignify a climate of research and enquiry which would justify the continued existence of a revived lodge of Guild operative masons working ceremonies said to have been those worked by the Guild masons of old, the Operatives might never have been able to attract members of sufficient quality and might easily have become a fruit which withered on the vine. "In short, historically the two societies have always been complementary, which is something that has consistently worked to their mutual advantage, and something worth remembering."[9]

The constituting of three more Assemblages

One thing is certain about the early days of this Society, which is that the prestigious and intellectual quality of its members, and their scholarly output, were such that, at least until the outbreak of World War II, there was never a shortage of candidates. In fact, from the Society's Register of Members 1914-1989 (recently returned to the Society) it is now known that during the first twenty years of its existence, Channel Row Assemblage indentured an average of over thirteen candidates per year, which is impressive given an entry requirement that candidates must already be members of Craft, Royal Arch and Mark Masonry. (N.B.That requirement has recently been modified, to accommodate masons in countries where Mark Masonry does not exist as a separate Order.)   A single lodge attracting such numbers today might be excused for considering itself fortunate indeed! Those figures also serve to explain Bernard Springett's 1931 appeal to Miss Bothwell-Gosse which began with the words "Our Channel Row Assemblage of Operative Masons is now so large ....." etc. (as described on pages 43-44). The inevitable consequence, of course, was a call for another Assemblage, and this was answered on 8th October, 1932 when a second Assemblage was founded for work in and around the Chelmsford area of Essex. It was constituted at 10 Duke Street, London and was named 'Friars Walk, Chelmersforde, Assemblage', taking its name from a pathway formerly used by Dominican Friars walking between their Priory and a well in Moulsham Street, Chelmsford. The Rev'd F.E. Crate was installed as its first Deputy Master Mason, and there were thirteen other founders.

Unfortunately the new Assemblage did not enjoy the immediate support accorded Channel Row Assemblage and a number of explanations have been suggested to account for the coolness of that response. They include resentment within the masonic community of Essex to anything new, especially coming from outside the Province; and the fact that, during its early years at least, the new Assemblage was inordinately reliant upon London masons for its ceremonial expertise, which was a source which began to dry up as war became inevitable and stopped entirely as soon as war was declared. Two more explanations were suggested by the Rev'd R.R.à-Ababrelton in his *Operative Review of 1941*, in which he he explained that "Meetings already arranged have had to be cancelled owing to enemy action, and the blackout has been a serious handicap". The author of this book, however, believes there may have been another, and more likely, reason for the new Assemblage's difficulties, which was that, despite their enthusiasm, too many of its Founders were unprepared for the workload involved in conducting most, if not all, of the seven ceremonies involved in operative free masonry. And, in that connection, it is worth noting that, prior to the constitution of the new Assemblage, all fourteen Founders had degrees 'conferred on them by name' (i.e. Without an accompanying ceremony). Six received three degrees in that way, four received two degrees, and four had one degree 'conferred' on them. They were, therefore, not the most experienced or best-prepared of lodge officers, having never seen all the operative ceremonies worked, even for themselves. In short, and despite the best of intentions on their part, in that particular Assemblage, and at that particular time, they were probably trying to go too far too soon. It is hardly surprising, therefore, that they fell at the first hurdle.

Whether one, two, or any of these explanations fully explains the difficulties Friars Walk Chelmersforde Assemblage encountered in its early days is now unknown. Nor is it known if they also suffered as a result of war-time travel restrictions to the Chelmsford area arising from the development of radar at the Marconi Works in that town. What *is* known is that a combination of factors undoubtedly worked to the disadvantage of the new Assemblage and it eventually became necessary for it to go into suspension for the duration of the war. In the event, that suspension lasted for thirty years, although there *was* a happy ending in that it was eventually 're-constituted', as will be explained in the next chapter.

Given the disappointing experience of the masons of Essex, it may seem strange that, in 1943, another Assemblage *was* successfully constituted, this time in London, and has survived ever since. The Assemblage concerned was Abbey Assemblage, which took its name from the 13th century Westminster Abbey and it was constituted on 9th February 1943. The difference between the experience of Abbey Assemblage and Friars Walk Chelmersforde Assemblage, however, was that -

since being constituted - the former has always met at the same location as Channel Row Assemblage which, since September 1972, has been Mark Masons' Hall in St. James's, London. For nearly thirty years prior to that the two Assemblages met at 10 Duke Street, St. James's, London. Thus, during the last two years of the War and the difficult years which followed, it was always possible for the officers of the two Assemblages to assist each other as far as working ceremonies was concerned and, in dire emergencies, meetings could always be amalgamated. Consequently, they both survived!

Only one other Assemblage was constituted during the Society's first fifty years, namely Kirkstall Abbey Assemblage, which was constituted at Leeds on 14th April, 1962. and took its name from a Cistercian Abbey founded in the 13th century. Like Friars Walk Chelmersforde Assemblage, its early years were difficult, not because of a lack of members, but because of its inability to find a permanent meeting place. As a result, it moved to Castleford in 1978, to Pontefract in 1990, and then back to Castleford again, all of which had an adverse effect on recruitment. Fortunately it eventually settled in York in 1997, since when it has never looked back, possibly because York has a long history of association with operative free masonry. (See N.B.Cryer's *York Mysteries Revealed*, Ian Allen Printing, 2006, which explains the York connection.)

The effect on freemasonry of the end of the 2nd World War

Although there was a regular supply of candidates prior to 1939, things changed dramatically during, and immediately after, the 2nd World War as the nation struggled to cope with the many social problems arising from such conflicts and the prolonged period of austerity which followed. They were difficult times and, as might be expected, freemasonry suffered accordingly, as explained by L.F.Elvin, a former 1st Grand Master Mason, who succinctly wrote "That war nearly killed us"; and R.J.Wilkinson (3rd Grand Master Mason in 1960) who, using words similar to those of Rev'd à-Ababrelton in his *Operative Review of 1941*, explained that: "The outbreak of the Second World War led to a difficult time, not only for our Order, but for Freemasonry in general. Blackout restrictions, travelling restrictions, the absence of its members with the forces or even on war work, catering troubles due to rationing and the requisitioning of masonic premises all tended to make meetings difficult and attendances uncertain."[10] Nor did those things end when the war ended. Clothes rationing didn't end until March 1949; petrol rationing didn't end until May 1950; and food rationing didn't end until July 1954, which can only have made masonic catering problematic. Potato rationing, in fact, did not even start until 1947!

The result for the Operatives was that, for several years, meetings were poorly attended, and those which were attended experienced ceremonies which, at best, can only be described as mediocre. Even worse, on some occasions, ceremonies were described rather than being worked in what is now the customary way. There were constant discussions concerning methods of injecting new life into the Society; the 1948 meeting of Grand Assemblage was so poorly attended that it was impossible to open a meeting, and those present used the time to discuss the calamitous state of the Society; the 1st Grand Master Mason repeatedly offered to resign so as to enable someone with more time to take over; and the Grand Clerk (J.H.Hack) *did* resign, citing as justification that "with failing health, the worries of lack of support from the powers-that-be made him feel that it would be better for the Order if a younger and more vigorous Brother took his place". All of which explains why R.F.B.Cross found it necessary to remain in office as 1st GMM from 1940 until his death in 1958; L.F.Elvin, served a total of eighteen years as 1st or 2nd Grand Master Mason, until his death in 1976; A.W.Dentith served as 2nd GMM from 1946 until 1954; E.B.Holmes served as 3rd GMM (which, it will be remembered, is a one-year appointment) for fifteen years, until his death in 1953; and J.H.Lawrance served for twenty-eight years as the Senior Past Master of Westminster Division, from 1932 until 1960.

Eventually, of course, a corner was turned and Freemasonry in general, and this Society in particular, began to revive. It was the start of a recovery which was long overdue, but from which the Society has never looked back. That having been explained, however, no member of the Operatives should ever lose sight of the depths of despair into which the Society descended after the 2nd World War, or the determination of a small group of stalwarts who kept it alive during the difficult and depressing post-war years. Fortunately, the next fifty years were less problematic and, after a slow beginning, eventually proved to be a sustained period of consolidation and expansion, as will become apparent in the next chapter.

REFERENCES

1. Peabody, D. 'Covent Garden and Freemasonry' in *Freemasonry Today* Issue 19, January 2002

2. Reddyhoff, J. W. *The Pallbearers of Matthew Birkhead* in AQC Vol. 105 (1992), pp. 192-194

3. Wright, T. D. 'The Craft in the British Isles in 1920' in *The Builder*, Vol. 7, No. 4 April 1921

4 à-Ababrelton, R. R. *The Operative Review No. 1* Dec. 1941

5 Bing, J. D. The Worshipful Society of Free Masons, Rough Masons, Wallers, Slaters, Paviors, Plaisterers and Bricklayers' in the *Transactions* of the Manchester Association for Masonic Research, Vol. LXV, 1975, pp. 24-36.

6 Carpenter, A. T. *John Theophilus Desagulier,* 2011, p. 225

7 In Memoriam in *The Speculative Mason,* Vol. LXV, 1954 & 1955, pp. 1-9

8 Rasoletti, J. and Lancee, E. *We three or three such as we* (2008)

9 Kibble-Rees, D. C. 'The Revival of the Operatives and their connection with the Masonic Study Society' in the MSS *Transactions*, Vol. LXXIX (2007), pp. 53-63

10 Wilkinson, R. J. *History of the Order of the Secret Monitor 1887 to 1963* (1964), pp. 26-27

CHAPTER 3

Consolidation and expansion (1964-2013)

The Society's second half-century was vastly different from its first and important events which occurred during those years include: The revival of the Society after the 2nd World War; expansion overseas; the appointment of Grand Assemblage officers; the purchase of a headquarters building; and the adoption of modern communications technology to facilitate the administration of the Society. As in the previous chapter, it is proposed to describe them under those sub-headings.

The revival of the Society after the 2nd World War

A welcome change in the fortunes of the Society came in the 1960s first - as already explained - with the constitution of Kirkstall Abbey Assemblage at Leeds, and then with that of Purbeck Quarries Assemblage at Wareham in Dorset. Wareham not only has an excellent masonic hall but the Isle of Purbeck, where it is located, has a well-documented history of association with the stone industry. There is a museum of the stone industry at Langton Matravers; the area's distinctive Portland stone can be seen in almost every cathedral in the country; and the Ancient Order of Purbeck Marblers and Stone Cutters has been active in the area for hundreds of years and still continues its ancient custom of kicking a football through the streets of Corfe Castle on

Shrove Tuesday, which is the day on which apprentices were traditionally indentured. It is also a harmless way of reminding locals of the industry's long-established right of way, which was of importance when the main method of transporting stone was by horse-drawn cart. So, all things considered, it is doubtful if the seed of operative free masonry planted at Wareham could have been sown in any more fertile ground unless, perhaps, it was at Chester, which was the intended location of the next Assemblage to be constituted, St. Werburgh Assemblage.

St. Werburgh is the ecclesiastical name of the cathedral in Chester and, when originally proposed, that was where it was intended a new Assemblage would be located because - like Wareham - it has a long history of association with stonemasonry and also with free masonry, as revealed by the Harleian MS No. 2054, explained by Randle Holme in 1688[1] and, more recently, by N. Barker Cryer[2]. In the event, however, events conspired against that decision. Its constitution in Liverpool had to be postponed because of 'industrial action' on the railways and, in the end, it was constituted at the National Liberal Club in London on 22nd July 1972, and eventually settled in Birkenhead, fifteen miles from Chester although, for a variety of reasons, it retained the name of St. Werburgh.

The following year Friars Walk, Chelmersforde, Assemblage was re-constituted at Southend-on-Sea, an Essex seaside town popular with Londoners. Its Founders were sixteen experienced freemasons who were more than capable of working the seven degrees of operative free masonry, and included Charles W.Marston (the last surviving member of the original Assemblage), Aynsley Andrews (a locally well-known manufacturer of masonic regalia), and Edwin George Gregory White (the masonic editor of The Times). This time the Assemblage prospered from the outset and, since that time, has acquired a reputation for the excellence of its ceremonies and its willingness to sponsor new Assemblages, such as Edmundsbury Abbey Assemblage at Bury St. Edmunds and St. Peter's Quarry Assemblage in Belgium, both of which were sponsored by the Assemblage in Southend.

A steady stream of other constitutions followed, including those of: Saint Helen Assemblage at Manchester (1977), Bodiam Castle Assemblage at Peacehaven (1977), Dudley Castle Assemblage at Birmingham (1980), Berry Head Quarry Assemblage at Brixham (1981), Loddon Bridge Assemblage at Wokingham (1983), Nonsuch Palace Assemlage at Sutton (1986), Castle Acre Assemblage at Watton(1986), Leeds Castle Assemblage at Gillingham (1986), Winchester Castle Assemblage at Winchester (1988), Waltham Abbey Assemblage at Chesham (1988), and Bodiniel Quarry Assemblage at Bodmin (1988) all of which continue to be well supported. In fact, apart from the suspension of Friars Walk, Chelmersforde, Assemblage during the 2nd World War, no Assemblage has ever found it necessary to return its Patent and, as explained, even that was only temporary. (A full list of Assemblages showing Constitution dates is provided at Appendix D)

Expansion overseas

Inevitably, news of the revival of operative free masonry and the existence of a Society charged with perpetuating its language and ceremonies, reached the furthermost corners of the masonic world, and enquiries began to be received regarding the possibility of Assemblages being constituted in countries other than England. First amongst those expressing such interest were the freemasons of Australia.

According to an account written at the time [3], news of the Society reached Australia by way of W.Bro Alan Martin of Melbourne, who had joined the Operatives in London thirty years earlier, and what he had to say, combined with what they had learned elsewhere, so aroused the interest of two particularly enthusiastic Australian freemasons, who were about to travel to London, that they made a point of being indentured to the Society on their arrival in the UK. They were Peter Green, who was indentured in October 1985, and Kent Henderson, who was indentured in April 1986, and both became members of Channel Row Assemblage. Expressed simply, both were actuated by a strong desire to see operative free masonry 'exported' to Australia.

Unfortunately, two problems arose to frustrate that objective which were that, according to the Society's Rules & Regulations, fourteen petitioners were (and still are) necessary before a new Assemblage can be considered; and new Assemblages can only be constituted by the three Grand Master Masons. That being the case, and bearing in mind that, at that time, there were only two (possibly three) members of the Society available to form an Assemblage in Australia, it was agreed that in the short term their best course of action would be to encourage other Australian freemasons to join the Society in the same way as they had done, i.e. as and when visiting the UK. This they set about encouraging, with the result that, within two years, a total of twenty Australian masons had joined the Society and progressed as far as the IV°.

Twenty being a viable number, within the normal course of events, the next step would have been for the three Grand Master Masons to travel to Australia to constitute an Assemblage there but, once again, fate dictated otherwise, and it was found impracticable for the three Grand Master Masons to travel at that time. Not wishing to lose momentum, plans were therefore drawn up for a number of the Australian members to fly to the UK so that an Australian Assemblage could be constituted in London for work in Melbourne. The name of the Assemblage was to be Chirnside Mansion Assemblage, after a local stately house, and the date of constitution was to be some time during the first week of April 1989.

As soon as news of the impending trip became known, however, what Henderson described as a masonic 'snowball' began to roll across Australia, other prospective candidates expressed a desire to join with them and, one way or another, a party of about one hundred brethren and their families eventually made its way to London for what became known as "Australia Week", which lasted from 1st - 7th April 1989. During that week, a further fifty-five Australian masons were indentured into the Society; Chirnside Mansion Assemblage was constituted on 3rd April; Eureka Quarries Assemblage was constituted on the morning of 5th April for work in Victoria, and Innisfallen Castle Assemblage was constituted later that same day, for work in New South Wales; Shenton's Mill Assemblage was constituted on 6th April for work in Western Australia; Bonython Hall Assemblage was constituted on the morning of 7th April for work in South Australia, and Bishopsbourne Assemblage was constituted later that day for work in Queensland. And, during the course of all this frenzied activity, Alan Williams was obligated as Senior Past Master, Peter

Green as Deputy Master V°, and Kent Henderson as Regional Clerk of what then became a 'Region' in its own right, i.e. Australia Region. In short, in one hectic week the Society had doubled its membership, and from that point on was active in two hemispheres! In Kent Henderson's words, "The whole exercise had been a magnificent example of fraternal co-operation across Australia, and across the world". But it didn't end there.

Two years later, and their early enthusiasm not having waned, the 1st Grand Master Mason and the Grand Clerk returned the compliment and flew to Australia to constitute three more Assemblages: Round House Assemblage at Fremantle on 1st October 1991; Invergowrie Homestead Assemblage at Melbourne on 4th October; and Murrindale Park Assemblage, also at Melbourne, on 5th October 1991. They then flew on to New Zealand, which had followed Australia's lead, where they constituted Belmont Quarries Assemblage on 12th October for work in Wellington; and Albert Barracks Assemblage on 14th October, for work in Auckland. Apart from the 1st Grand Master Mason (D.R.Stuckey) all principal offices were filled by Australian masons, Alan Williams and Peter Green being 'commissioned' to perform the roles of 2nd and 3rd Grand Master Masons respectively.

It is not proposed to go into further detail concerning the many Assemblages constituted after that date, and it is hoped that it will be sufficient to add that, during the next twenty-two years, a further seventy-eight Assemblages were constituted, six more in Australia, one in Belgium, four in Bolivia, three in Brazil, one in Canada, two in France, two in Hong Kong, five in India, two in Malaysia, three more in New Zealand, one in Singapore, three in South Africa, two in Spain, five in the USA, and thirty-eight more in England and Wales, bringing the total number of Assemblages to one hundred and eight. To put that in context, by the end of its first fifty years, the Society had two Assemblages; by the end of its second fifty years, it had another one hundred and six, which speaks volumes for the increasing popularity of operative free masonry.

The appointment of Grand Officers

For many years after 1931, which was the year that Channel Row Assemblage re-invented itself as a national society, there was virtually no requirement for Grand officers apart from assisting with constitution ceremonies and the annual meeting of Grand Assemblage and, on those occasions, whatever duties became necessary were performed by the corresponding officers of Channel Row Assemblage.

In 1982, however, Derek Stuckey was appointed Grand Clerk and, wisely anticipating the continuing expansion of the Society, he decided that, in the long run, the Society would not only require a team of Grand Officers but, eventually, would also require a headquarters of its own. He therefore made a start by recruiting W.R. (Bill) Box, who eventually succeeded him as Grand Clerk.   More importantly, he also provided office space (above a shop) in one of the properties he owned near Kings Cross station, as a headquarters, where a team of Grand officers could meet and work together for the future development of the Society. Over time, that team gradually increased to include a Grand Treasurer, Registrar, Bursar, Librarian, Outside Guard, a number of Deputies, and a Grand Master Masons' 'Superintendent of Work', who thereafter performed the duties previously carried out by a Director of Ceremonies. Bill Box remained in office until 2000. Derek Stuckey served six years as Grand Clerk, and then a further eleven years as he progressed through the ranks of 3rd, 2nd and 1st Grand Master Mason, i.e. a total of seventeen years at the highest level. In retrospect, as far as this Society is concerned, it is almost impossible to overstate the importance the two of them played in shaping the modern Society and raising its profile to that which it enjoys today. (A list of Grand Officers is attached at Appendix B.)

The purchase of a headquarters building

Their crowning achievement was the setting-up of a Footing Corner Stone Fund, so as to accumulate sufficient funds to finance the purchase (and future maintenance) of a property suitable for use as the Society's headquarters. This they set in motion at Grand Assemblage in 1990, following which the Fund was declared the only official charity of the Society and members (and Assemblages) were invited to donate to it, either by direct gift or bank 'standing order'. Differing levels of contribution were acknowleged by the wearing of distinctive badges (i.e. Gold, Silver, Bronze or Iron) and these were later supplemented by the introduction of a Great Corner Stone Award breast jewel for those members whose personal contribution amounted to £1000 or more and it is considered noteworthy that many members of the Society, and one Assemblage, have since qualified for that award. The Assemblage concerned is Bodiam Castle Assemblage which, by the end of September 2012 had donated £22,535 to the Fund.

Although neither Derek Stuckey nor Bill Box lived long enough to see the fruit of their labours, donations to the fund had reached such a level that, on 9th January 2009, the Society was able to purchase (and later renovate) the Masonic Rooms at 166 Great North Road, The Green, Eaton Socon, St. Neots, Cambridgeshire, which henceforth became the headquarters of the Society. That purchase, more than anything else, ensured that the contribution made by Derek Stuckey and Bill Box to the development of this Society would never be forgotten. Whether that was their intention or not, is immaterial. The fact is that, by the creation of an administrative team and the purchase of a headquarters, they left their mark on this Society, which is something masons have been doing to the structures they built, for centuries.

The new headquarters at Eaton Socon.

The Masonic Rooms at Eaton Socon are now managed by a Premises Committee, the chairman of which is Rt.W.Bro.Peter Fotheringham, OSOM, who not only worked unceasingly to bring the acquisition about, but has continued to labour thereafter to transform the building into a headquarters worthy of the Society.

The adoption of modern communications technology to facilitate the administration of the Society.

When the author of this book succeeded Bill Box as Grand Clerk in September 2000 there was still a need for an administrative headquarters. The rooms at 20 Caledonian Road provided by Derek Stuckey consisted of a bedroom, an office, a conference room (about the size of a domestic dining room), a kitchen, a small amount of storage space in the attic for files, and more in the cellar for equipment and furniture, such as pedestals and floor gauges. It invariably seemed inadequate when staff were called in to prepare 'mail shots' to Assemblages, or when working on the Directory or Annual Returns, and it was decidedly over-crowded when used for the many meetings which the previous Grand Clerk thought necessary, such as Grand Master Masons' meetings, 'Admin Team' meetings, separate meetings of Senior Passed Masters, and of Regional Clerks (all of which involved meals) plus Lodges of Instruction as and when the necessity arose. And it would be an understatement to say that, on those occasions, the thought of one day owning a building, where meetings could be held in comfort, was an enticing prospect.

Times change, however, and the administration of the Society today is conducted in a totally different manner from that which was customary in the days of Derek Stuckey and Bill Box mainly because, during the interim period, there had been a revolution in communications technology. In 1990 correspondence was invariably despatched by post (which was expensive and slow), and the favoured form of face-to-face communication between Grand officers and middle-management was by meetings, either weekly, monthly or quarterly, and frequently involved journies of hundreds of miles. In 2012 the quickest and cheapest form of communication is by e.mail or text (which are instantaneous and inexpensive) and the easiest forms of face-to-face communication are by skype, 'conference call' or some form of 'social interactive network', none of which involve travelling. A similar revolution has taken place in the world of document storage and retrieval. In 1990 archives were stored in filing cabinets or on shelves. In 2012, however, files are stored electronically and, whether accurate or not, one regularly hears comments such as "the contents of the British Library could be stored in a shoe-box" if one so wished! Libraries and museums have obviously been affected by this revolution and, in 2012, books can be bought or borrowed in e.book or ibook form, and it is no longer necessary to go on some form of 'Grand Tour' to see historic places or buildings, or necessary to visit museums in order to see or examine exhibits, many museums providing 'virtual tours' which can be taken on any day and at any time, in the comfort of one's home.

Not wishing to unduly protract this explanation of the changes which have taken place during the last twenty years, it is hoped that it will be sufficient to briefly remind readers that people today not only store hours of music on their mobile phones, but many also have hundreds of books available at the touch of a button, and electronic readers, notebooks and tablets come pre-loaded with encyclopaedias, dictionaries. and the complete works of Shakespeare and Dickens. Even the one-time marvel of the laptop computer is now looked on as outmoded and already something of a relic. All of which hopefully explains why it is that the day-to-day administration of this Society is not now carried out at the Society's headquarters but, in the main, is conducted electronically. Apart from the Grand Bursar, who is obliged to store certain items (i.e. Rituals and Directories) on shelves, much of the work is comfortably conducted from the Grand Clerk's home.

Two brief examples will amplify this phenomon for anyone doubting the speed and extent of the communications revolution which has taken place during the past twenty or thirty years. When the author of this book became Grand Clerk in 2000, he was delighted to be able to produce an A4-folded leaflet explaining the aims and background of the Society, which could be put on display in masonic halls and libraries for the benefit of anyone wishing to find out more about the Society. With the aid of the Grand Bursar, he also produced a computer-disk of all the Society's forms and letter-heads, which was distributed to all Regional and Assemblage clerks so as to ensure that the Society's forms and correspondence reflected well on the Society's image. Both of those innovations have long since disappeared, and everything they contained is better illustrated and more easily available on the Society's interactive website.

As has already been said, and was recently emphasised by the Grand Secretary of the United Grand Lodge of England in an article concerning masonic websites[4].... times change!

REFERENCES

1. Holme, R. III The Academie of Armourie (1688)

2. Cryer, N. B. *The Restoration Lodge of Chester* (The Cornerstone Society) 2002

3. Henderson, K. *The Australian connection - How it happened* published privately by the Society in 1989

4. Brown, N. Digital Delivery in *Freemasonry Today*, No. 16, Winter 2011, p. 24

CHAPTER 4

Some distinguishing characteristics of the Society

Most, but not all, of the explanations which follow are taken from the books of Thomas Carr[1] and Charles H. Merz[2] who were contemporaries of Stretton. It is not proposed to provide any further amplification other than to draw the reader's attention to the fact that Dr. Carr's book begins with an extract from the Minutes of a meeting of operative Lodge "Mount Bardon" No. 110 held on 6th May 1911, which recorded the following important resolution:

"That the paper written by Thomas Carr of 9 Carlton Terrace, Blackpool, M.D., on 'The Ritual of the Operative Free Masons' is a true and accurate account of the ceremonies practiced by this Lodge, and that the tradition which has been handed down to us is that these ceremonies have been so practised from time immemorial. That the said paper is based upon information furnished by us or by our accredited members and that the said Thomas Carr has received our permission to publish the said paper."

That declaration is signed by John A.Grant (1st Master), Robert Walter Grant (2nd Master), William George Major Bailey (3rd Master), and Robert B. Grant, Secretary, IPM, VII° (N.B. Robert Bennett Grant was the long-serving Superintendent of the Granite Quarries at Bardon, and Robert Walter Grant was his son, also employed at the Quarries[3].)

ANTIENT DRAMA

The Antient Drama is a ceremony performed at Grand Assemblage each year, designed to commemorate the heroic death of Hiram Abiff, who was slain after the completion of King Solomon's Temple because of his refusal to dislose the secrets of a Master Mason. It is a ceremony of great importance to operative masons. It requires a cast of twenty-two, a substantial amount of equipment, and a room of considerable size. Because the 3rd Grand Master Mason plays the part of Hiram Abiff, the Antient Drama is the device used by Operatives to replace their 3rd Grand Master Mason at the end of his one-year term of office.

APPRENTICES

'Candidates' for operative free masonry are rarely described as such but as 'apprentices', and they do not 'join' the Operatives but are 'indentured' (see below) for seven years which, since 1356, has been the length of time thought necessary to learn a trade (Carr p.28, and Knoop and Jones[4]). Irrespective of their actual age, therefore, all 'apprentices' represent a youth of about 14 or 15 years of age, who is seeking to become a stonemason. He is symbolically required to post his application at the door of a quarry or lodge and "on three occasions, stand by his application when the men are going to and from work so that all may see him; and if any one knows anything against him they must report it at the office" (Carr, p.21).

ASHLARS

According to Merz (p.147) "In the Operative lodge room, there are always the Rough Ashlar, the Rough Dressed Ashlar and the Perfect Ashlar The Rough Ashlar is the cube stone as it leaves the quarry and it is placed in the First Degree Stone-yard. It is in the rough state as it has been 'rough hewn' by cowans or 'scabblers'. These men are not Free Masons and use only the pointed scabbling hammer. The Apprentices and Masons in the First Degree work with a three-quarter inch round headed chisel and make the stone 'rough dressed', preparing it for the hands of the more expert Craftsmen. The Fellows of the Craft in the Second Degree receive the 'Rough Dressed' Ashlar and work upon it with their one and one-half inch chisels and then rub the stone down until it becomes a Perfect Ashlar. This Ashlar is then sent to the Third Degree stone-yard where it is properly marked by the Mark Masons..." and then sent to the site to be placed in position by the Erectors. Modern Operatives moralise on these ashlars which are used extensively in their ceremonies.

ASSEMBLAGES

Operative free masons meet in Assemblages which take their name from Article 23 of an Ancient Charge given to a Fellow of the Craft which stipulates that masons must attend their annual Assembly. They consist of joint meetings of lodges, the most common of which are Assemblages of Lodges I° - IV°. Both Rev. James Anderson and William Preston referred to 'Assemblies' of freemasons rather than lodges.

CENTRAL PEDESTAL

The Holy Book in a lodge of operative masons (like those in Royal Arch, the Order of the Secret Monitor, and Craft lodges in Ireland and parts of the north east of England) is located on a pedestal in the centre of the lodge, not on the Master's pedestal at the front of a lodge. It is surrounded by a rectangle of carpet (laid out in the proportions 3:1) which is referred to as the 'candidate's track' and is said to represent the foundations of King Solomon's Temple. That portion of the lodge within that rectangle is considered 'Holy Ground', and members are not permitted to walk thereon unless it is covered. The Holy Book itself is only touched during meetings to change pages (depending on the degree being worked) and those members needing to hold a Bible in their hands in order to take an Obligation are provided with a separate copy, which they support on their open left hand, their right hand resting on top, in a manner well known to the freemasons of Scotland, where there is a well-documented history of operative free masonry.

FYLFOT CROSS

For centuries before Hitler hijacked it, the Fylfot Cross - also known as the swastika - was important to Guild operative masons, being a universal emblem of good fortune. It is still to be seen in cathedrals, on furniture, on ornaments and on church vestments throughout the British Isles and is also used by societies, such as the Golden Dawn and the Theosophists. In ancient Guild masonry a Fylfot Cross was placed on the floor of the lodge and, today, a small representation (made from four masons' "squares") is placed on the Bible on the central pedestal. It is sometimes decribed as a *gammadion* because a mason's square closely resembles the Greek letter gamma, and F.W.Seal Coon explains the ceremonial use of a gammadion in his explanation of a Guild 'Old-Time Midsummer Ceremony'[5]. A further explanation, linking it to the Pole Star and the letter 'G' is provided in 'Liberal Arts and Sciences' below.

GAUGES

One of the unique features of the Operatives is that its members are themselves regarded as "Living Stones" being prepared to eventually take their place in a spiritual house, "that house not made by hands, eternal in the heavens" (2 Corinthians 5:1). That being so, as they progress through the various grades, they are physically 'tested' at each stage by being examined against a full-size gauge, each of which is a template of a type of stone used in building, such as an Ashlar Square stone, a Running stone, an Elbow Square stone, or a Footing Corner stone, depending on the grade being worked

An Assemblage's gauges

On the face of it, this may suggest an opportunity for frivolity, but such is never the case. The two Wardens quietly approach each candidate, who is asked to step into the gauge, which is then lifted over his head whilst the Super Intendent of Work confirms that "The candidate passes the test". It is a serious part of the ceremony which is always carried out with dignity and candidates are invariably pleased that, in the eyes of their fellows, they are making progress in the Society.

GRAND MASTER MASONS

Three Grand Master Masons setting out the ground plan.

According to the Rules of the Society, the three Grand Master Masons are the only members of the VII° Lodge and all other members of that degree are described only as 'VII° *honoris causa*'. Like the officers of Royal Arch, they represent Solomon (King of Israel), Hiram (King of Tyre), and Hiram Abiff, but Dr. Carr claims they can also be identified with the Grand Master, Pro Grand Master, and Deputy Grand Master of Craft masonry. They carry rods (not sceptres) which measure 5, 4 and 3 units respectively (it doesn't matter whether they are five feet or five cubits) and they are coloured blue, red and black for reasons explained by Plutarch. Writers have likened them to the virga geometricalis (i.e. measuring rods) of Roman architects, and the rope-stretchers (harpedonaptae) of Ancient Egypt, who tied knots at 3, 4 and 5 unit intervals for the purpose of creating right-angled triangles. They are used for setting out the ground for a new building, by way of the Theorem of Pythagoras. For some years it was the custom for Grand Master Masons on appointment to sign a "Triangular agreement" (see Merz p.197) to work together (i.e. The Rule of Three) although that custom is no longer observed.

HEXAGONAL PEDESTALS

The three most important officers of an operative lodge are the Deputy Master Mason and Deputies Jachin and Boaz. They sit at hexagonal pedestals, which are located at the points of an equilateral triangle (an emblem of the Deity) the internal angles of which are all 60° (i.e. a total of 180°). The points of that triangle represent the three Biblical mountains, Moriah, Tabor and Sinai, and the officers themselves represent the King, Church and State 'in union'. Deputy Jachin acts as the lodge Chaplain, and Deputy Boaz acts as its Doctor and Almoner. All three are appointed annually by the three Grand Master Masons and must have attained the VI°. The hexagon (like the square and triangle) is an important geometrical figure for operative masons, and its corners have been associated with those of the Hexalpha (i.e. Seal of Solomon) which, in days gone by, was extensively used as a Mark by operative masons. It is also reflected in Metatron's Cube, which is a figure in sacred geometry. At one time a hexagon was shown on the floor cloth of Mark masons, and newly obligated Mark

Masters were told that it referred to the six equiangular triangles which form a regular hexagon. It still forms an important role in the Royal Arch and is depicted on the jewel of the Order and described in the Lecture on that Jewel contained in the Aldersgate ritual which, interestingly, links it to the Operative masons of 1701.

INDENTURE

An indenture is a legal agreement between two or more parties binding one into the service of another, such as would be signed by an apprentice (or servant) and his employer. As a document it takes it name from the fact that it is in two parts, each part having corresponding indented edges for identification and security, and each party retains one half. The form used in the Society today is identical to those used by apprentices a century ago, at which time they were purchased from Waterlow & Sons Ltd. of London Wall. Dr. Merz's Indenture is reproduced on page 3 of his book *Guild Masonry in the Making*.

JABAL

Although only briefly described in the Bible as the son of Lamech and the founder of those who dwell in tents and have liverstock, Jabal is a name which looms large in operative free masonry (Merz,p.12), he being "the first man to build a house of stone" and consequently the founder of building and architecture. He is referred to in most of the Ancient Charges and in the *Fellowcraft's Song* written by Charles de La Faye whch was included in Anderson's *Constitutions* of 1723.

KEYS

Keys used to be an important item on Tracing Boards but have now largely disappeared from speculative masonic ritual. They are still important in operative free masonry, however, and the Ceremony of the Keys is an important part at the opening and closing of any Assemblage meeting. The Master Masons are said to have sat on a throne with seven steps, each step of which represented one of the Seven Liberal Arts and Sciences. The 'steps' were actually archives of the secrets of operative free masonry, and each step was secured by means of three locks. It was necessary for all three Master Masons to be present and in possession of their keys, before a meeting could begin. The transfer of the key from around the neck of the slain Hiram Abiff, to his successor as 3rd Grand Master Mason, is an important part of the Ancient Drama re-enacted at Grand Assemblage each year.

LIBERAL ARTS AND SCIENCES

The seven Liberal Arts and Sciences were considered of great importance by operative masons, which is why they are mentioned in all the Ancient Charges[6], and why speculative freemasonry has preserved a memorial of that importance in the Fellowcraft's degree and the Inner Working of a Board of Installed Masters. For centuries they were considered to be the total sum of human knowedge and, according to Merz (p. 295) the trivium and quadrivium formed the basis of all that used to be taught in schools and universities. The trivium concerned language, and included Grammar, Rhetoric and Logic, and the quadrivium concerned mathematics, and included Arithmetic, Geometry, Music and Astronomy. As far as the operatives were concerned, by far the most important of these was Geometry and, in the Halliwell MS, it is claimed that Geometry and Masonry are synonymous, which is the reason that the letter 'G' is prominent in lodges. The importance of geometry would also seem to be demonstrated by the continuing inclusion of the five regular Platonic solids in the ritual of the Royal Arch, and the illustration of the 47th Proposition of Euclid on a Past Masters collar in the Craft. Astronomy was important to the early operatives because new buildings were 'set out' by the Master Masons from a centre aligned from the Pole Star, which was regarded as the most stable star in the sky. They also had an interest in the axial rotation of the Great Bear around the Pole Star, which they symbolised in their lodges with a swastika (or, as it is known in this country, a Fylfot Cross) which - for centuries - was universally regarded as a symbol of Good Fortune. It is possibly worth adding that, for practical reasons, the corner stone of all new buildings was traditionally fixed in the north east, and masonic halls are to this day adorned with astronomical and astrological symbols which are difficult to explain unless the importance of astronomy to free masonry is understood and accepted.

ORIENTATION

Operative lodges are orientated west to east (i.e. with the senior officers sitting in the west.) This is because King Solomon's Temple was orientated that way with the Holy of Holies in the west and the two great pillars (Jachin and Boaz) in the east. The Deputy Master in the Operatives sits in the west so that he can see the sun rising in the east and thereby knows when to start work; the Senior Warden sits in the east so that he can see the setting sun at the close of day; and the Junior Warden sits in the north so that he can see the sun at its meridian. Contrary to popular opinion, not all cathedrals and churches are orientated east to west. St. Paul's Church in Covent Garden was built west to east by Inigo Jones, the celebrated architect and Grand Master of operative free masonry. St. Paul's Basilica in the Vatican, and the Basilica of the Resurrection at Jerusalem were also built with a west to east orientation. The altar of Coventry Cathedral is actually in the north which, to avoid controversy, is regarded as the "liturgical east" of the cathedral.

REGALIA

Operative free masons wear little regalia. An apprentice wears only a blue cord around his neck, but 2nd, 3rd and 4th degree members suspend a small 'jewel' from that cord, indicating their rank in operative masonry.

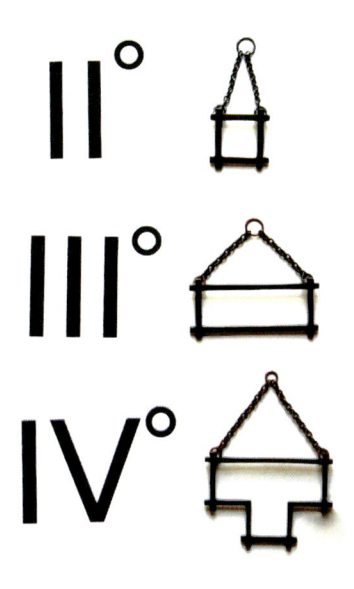

II°

III°

IV°

Degree 'jewels'.

5th, 6th and 7th degree members wear collarettes, from which they suspend the jewel of their rank, and the three Grand Master Masons also wear academic robes and bicorn hats, similar to those worn by the corresponding officers of Livery Companies. All regalia is the property of the Society.

RELIGION

It will be remembered that both Major Gorham and the Revd. S.S.Stitt considered operative free masonry to be a "Religion and Trade combined" (pp.21-22) and, whilst not being prepared to support that view entirely, the author of this book is in no doubt that religion occupies an important part in the ritual of the Society, from start to finish. Meetings begin and end with prayers to the Great Architect of Heaven and Earth, and additional prayers are offered at the start of grade ceremonies and sealed (at the end) on the Volume of the Sacred Law. The word 'God' is rarely used, other than as part of the Society's motto "God is our guide", its members preferring to address the Deity as 'El Shaddai', which is Hebrew for Almighty God (Genesis 16:7) and may be interpreted gematrially as 345, a figure of importance to operative masons. The most striking characteristic of operative masonry, however, is the Sevenfold Salute to the Most High which is given silently and addressed to the Most High at various points in a meeting, and involves a series of co-ordinated moves revolving around geometric shapes, most of which are triangles.

SEVEN DEGREE SYSTEM

The modern Operatives maintain a logical and coherent system of progression designed to reflect the programme of training followed by the original Guild. Its seven-stages are: Entered Apprentice, Fellow of the Craft, Fitter & Marker, Setter Erector, Super Intendent & Overseer, Passed Master, and Grand Master Mason. There are specific time limits between each level and candidates for progression are (symbolically) required to produce a specimen of their work, have the approval of their Super Intendent of Work, and pass the test of the appropriate Gauge (see above), before progressing further. There are Passing Words, grips and signs of recognition between each grade, and ceremonies are always accompanied by a Lecture designed to explain some aspect of the work and traditions of their Guild predecessors, all of which also explains why - in the Operatives - members of the VI° are known as 'Passed Masters' rather than 'Past Masters'. In the Operatives they will have passed all the necessary stages leading to that grade. It is also considered important that there is no form of age barrier (whether official or unofficial) as far as progression is concerned, and it is a feature of the Society of which they are proud, that any member who has attained the VI° and is still active at the age of ninety, is eligible for promotion to the highest grade of the Society, i.e. that of VII° Honoris Causa. About four or five members of the Society are promoted to that grade, in that way, every year, and all continue to support the Society thereafter with energy and enthusiasm.

SUPER INTENDENT OF WORK

The post of Super Intendent of Work is a unique appointment in an Assemblage and it would be a mistake to regard his duties as identical to those of a Director of Ceremonies in any other Order or Society. He is the custodian of, and the one who sets-out, all equipment and furnishings, the officer who maintains the standard of work, and (unlike speculative freemasonry) the person who 'stands in' for the Deputy Master if he is unable to be present. As a result, he is - in every sense of the word - the most expert craftsman in an Assemblage.

A Super Intendent of Work's table

He is seated in the south, directly opposite the Junior Warden, and has a table which is invariably covered by a mass of chisels, mauls, keys, rulers, plumb-lines, working plans, ashlars, templates and gauges, plus - of course - the full-size 'working tools' (i.e. square, level and plumb-rule) of the Assemblage, and sufficient carpet (or cloth) to produce a floor-plan of a temple, in the ratio of 3:1. In short, it is an appointment suited only to the most capable of ritualists and the fittest of men.

TRUNCHEONS

The principal officers of an Assemblage use truncheons to call for order, not gavels. This is not because gavels are new as items of furniture but because they had no place in quarries or stonemasons' lodges. Truncheons, on the other hand, have been symbols of authority for centuries. At the State funeral of

Cromwell, for instance, the Knight Marshal and his Deputy carried truncheons and, today, when the Lord Chancellor leaves the House of Lords on official duty, he is preceded by a Tipstaff carrying such a symbol of his authority. In days gone by, parish constables would leave their truncheons outside to show that they were 'at home', and would occasionally send a truncheon to the scene of a disturbance, when they were unable to attend in person. In operative free masonry, of course, especially when the Wardens stand up to "bar progress" to an apprentice during his circuits around the lodge, the truncheon is a far more impressive and convenient symbol of authority than would be either a hammer, mallet or gavel. At least, so thought the early Guild masons who adopted it and so think the modern Operatives who continue the practice.

REFERENCES

1 Carr, T. *The ritual of the Operative Free Masons* (1911) published by Tyler Publishing Company

2 Merz, C. J. *Guild Masonry in the Making* (1918) published by the Light Publishing Company

3 Fenn, R. W. D. *The Bardon Hill Quarries - 1 1858 - 1918* (an unpublished paper, available on-line) - p. 14

4 Knoop, D. and Jones, G. P. Masons in the Middle Ages in *Ars Quatuor Coronatorum,* Vol. 98, (1985), pp. 90-108

5 Seal-Coon, F. W. Op. Cit, pp. 166-171

6 Mackey, A. G. *The History of Freemasonry* (The Masonic History Company), Vol. 1, pp. 40-43

CHAPTER 5

The Grand Master Masons

Until 19th October 1931 when Channel Row Assemblage re-invented itself as a 'sovereign' (i.a. self-governing and independent) masonic Society, there was no need for Grand Master Masons or, for that matter, any other sort of Grand Officer. It had three Master Masons and a Deputy Master Mason to work its ceremonies, it was supervised by a Court of Assistants and, throughout its early years, no other tiers of management were thought necessary.

But they soon became necessary thereafter, primarily for constituting new Assemblages and presiding at annual meetings of Grand Assemblage although, as has been explained elsewhere, "from 1931 until the mid-seventies it was not unusual for Grand Master Masons - sometimes all three - not to attend Grand Assemblage or, confusingly, for other members of the VII° to deputise for them on official visits, signing their names in Attendance Registers and even on certificates, as the actual office holders."[1] In that connection, however, it is worth remembering that between 1933 and 1960, the average attendance at Grand Assemblage was only eighteen and, in 1948, was only six, probably because, during its early years, Grand Assemblage had not yet attained the position of importance in the Society's calendar that it now enjoys.

Today, of course, the responsibilities of the Grand Master Masons are considerably more onerous and, in addition to the tasks just mentioned, now include the day-to-day administration of an international organisation; the husbandry of a substantial budget; the maintenance of relations with other masonic Orders and Societies; the appointment and supervision of Grand and Regional officers to administer the Society; a demanding programme of 'official visits' to Assemblages and Regions; and the maintenance and further development of its headquarters at Eaton Socon. As a consequence, their burden, especially that on 1st Grand Master Masons, has increased considerably and now necessitates international air travel (always by the cheapest routes possible) involving expense, time away from one's family, work and other responsibilities, and possibly harm to one's health arising from medical conditions such as Deep Vein Thrombosis and the Avian flu epidemic which the author encountered on a trip to the Far East. And it should never be thought that such visits are "perks of the job", as anyone knows who has taken a long-haul flight and then been expected to carry out four or five days of degree ceremonies, followed by the physically-demanding constitution of three or four new Assemblages. In short, it is not an appointment to be undertaken lightly, and there can sometimes be an element of personal sacrifice involved.

Given those facts, it is proposed to provide a few biographical details concerning three of the more recent 1st GMMs for the benefit of future members of the Society who might wonder what it takes to become eligible for such a position, starting with Derek Stuckey because, as explained in Chapter 3, it was he who first recognised the necessity for a Society headquarters and an administrative 'team' to run it.

Derek Richard Stuckey was born on 5th October 1916 at 2 Keystone Crescent, Kings Cross, London which was one of several houses built in the area by his grandfather. He moved to Berkshire as a child and did not live in Keystone Crescent again until the death of his mother in the early 1960s following which he moved back again to take over the family business. He died on 19th September 2007, at which time he owned a number of properties in and around Keystone Crescent, nine shops in the Caledonian Road, and was a Director of the Beech Hill Jersey Herd Limited at Burghfield Common, Reading. By profession he was a Barrister, with chambers at No. 3 Dr. Johnson's Buildings in the Temple.

As far as freemasonry was concerned, he was a member of Old Bradfield Lodge No. 3549 and Gray's Inn Lodge No. 4938. He also joined a number of other masonic Orders and Societies, including the Societas Rosicruciana in Anglia (in which he attained the 9°) and the Order of Eri. He was 'indentured' into Operative free masonry in Abbey Assemblage on 14th November 1972 and became Grand Clerk ten years later, 3rd Grand Master Mason in 1987, 2nd Grand Master Mason from 1988-1990, and 1st Grand Master Mason from 1991 until 1998, i.e. a total of seventeen years at the highest level of the Society.

As already explained, his particular legacy as far as the Operatives are concerned is that it was he who realised that, because of the expansion of the Society, it would eventually require a headquarters of its own, for which purpose he created the Footing Corner Stone Fund (see page 63) so as to be able to purchase such a property if and when the opportunity should arise.

In the short term, however, he provided temporary accommodation over one of his shops in the Caledonian Road and began the process of creating a team of officers to run it, which included William Reginald Box, who was his Grand Clerk for eleven years, and Nigel Alan Willows, who was his Grand Treasurer for ten years.

Derek Stuckey was succeeded as 1st Grand Master Mason by Arthur Craddock, who was born in Ilkeston, Derbyshire on 6th March 1933. Sadly, both of his parents died before he was nine years of age, so it hardly surprising that, at the earliest opportunity, he enlisted as a Boy Soldier, following which the army became his 'family'. He enjoyed the military life and has frequently expressed his gratitude for the education he received at its hands, and the manner in which it instilled in him the qualities of self-discipline, compassion and respect for others. He was rapidly promoted and thoroughly enjoyed the opportunities presented for widening his experience and for foreign travel. In 1956, he was initiated into freemasonry in the United Services Lodge No. 3813 in Gibraltar. Freemasonry obviously satisfied a 'need' in his life because he then went on to join the Royal Arch, Mark, and various other Orders and, in 1959, he left the army and joined the staff at Mark Masons' Hall so as to make freemasonry a lifetime career. He worked there for thirty-two years and eventually became Deputy Grand Secretary, being only the second 'in house' member-of-staff to attain that honour.

Needless to say he took an active part in all the Orders administered by Mark Masons' Hall, as well as others such as the Military and Hospitaller Order of St. Lazarus of Jerusalem, and the Venerable Order of St. John of Jerusalem. In the Order of St. Lazarus he became a Knight Grand Cross and Bailiff of the Grand

Bailiwick of England, and in the Order of St. John he became a Serving Brother (S.B.St.J.) and then an Officer (O.St.J.). He also joined the Societas Rosicruciana in Anglia, in which he became the Senior Substitute Magus, the Royal Order of Eri, the August Order of Light, and the Antient and Accepted Rite (Rose Croix) in which he attained the 32º. He also served for six years as Deputy Grand Master of the Allied Masonic Degrees, and fifteen years as the Provincial Grand Master of the Royal Order of Scotland in Hertfordshire.

As far as the Operatives were concerned he became 3rd Grand Master Mason in 1989, 2nd Grand Master Mason from 1991 until 1994, and 1st Grand Master Mason from 1998 until 1st May 2011 when he felt compelled to resign because of a 'stroke' which limited his mobility. The Society was fortunate to have had such an experienced freemason at its head for such a long time, but the role of 1st Grand Master Mason is physically demanding and Arthur was the first to realise that it was time to make way for a younger and fitter man.

Fortunately there was someone available with those qualifications, namely Nigel Alan Willows, who was not only young enough to cope with the pressures involved but had already spent ten years as Grand Treasurer, eleven years as a Deputy Grand Master Mason and Senior Past Master, and one year as 3rd Grand Master Mason. Moreover, he had taken part in several trips abroad during which he carried out the duties of either 2nd or 3rd Grand Master Mason (as required), so he was well aware of what was involved in accepting the role.

By profession he is the UK Controller and Company Secretary of an international company producing satellite-based navigation, positioning and communication data with a global turnover of over £2 billion. In freemasonry he is the son of a freemason, a member of most other Orders and Societies, and his hobbies are steam traction and model railways, overseas travel, and supporting Chelsea Football Club.

Tempting though it may be, it is not intended to provide further background information on any of the previous 1st Grand Master Masons, because the nature of the role has changed so much during the last twenty-five years, and how anyone coped with the responsibility of that office beforehand is of little relevance to that which is experienced today.

A complete list of all the Grand Master Masons who have served the Society, from 1931 to the present day, is provided at Appendix A.

REFERENCE

1   Kibble-Rees, D. C. *The Operatives* (Lulu Publishing) 2009, p. 45

CHAPTER 6

A toast to the Founders

Midnight on the 20th May 2013 will mark the completion of one hundred years in the life of the Operatives, and a century in almost any walk of life is a considerable achievement. In days gone by, for example, anyone approaching their one hundredth birthday could look forward to a telegram from the Queen congratulating them on their longevity. In the same way, a cricketer scoring his one hundredth 'run' could look forward to a standing ovation and handshakes all round. In short, it is - and always has been - an achievement worthy of celebration.

So it is in freemasonry for those lodges and chapters able to prove an uninterrupted existence for one hundred years. They are encouraged to celebrate the occasion with some sort of event, the lodge is presented with a commemorative Centenary Warrant, and its members thereafter are permitted to wear a distinctive breast-jewel marking their achievement, irrespective of whether they have been members for fifty years or fifty minutes. Doubtless, on a convenient date near to the 21st May 2013 the Operatives will do the same and, at some point in their celebrations, a toast will be proposed and glasses will be raised to 'The Founders'.

Before doing so, however, it is hoped that a thought will also be spared for those who were not Founders but did just as much to ensure the success of a Society which started in 1913 with eleven members in an obscure London theatre but now has more than three thousand members in fifteen different countries, all of whom have one thing in common, i.e. A firm belief that freemasonry is older and bigger than was claimed in 1813 when, for reasons that were thought necessary at the time, it was solemnly - but incorrectly - pronounced that: 'Pure Ancient Masonry consists of three degrees and no more, viz. those of the Entered Apprentice, the Fellow Craft, and the Master Mason, including the Supreme Order of the Holy Royal Arch.'

This is neither the time nor the place to argue that case, but it is most certainly the time for acknowledging the debt that the modern Operatives owe to those who shared that belief and were determined that speculative freemasons would never forget the part the operative free masons (and especially the Guild masons) played in the success of their fraternity. Men like Clement Edwin Stretton and John Yarker whose early enthusiasm brought the Society into being; and those writers and lecturers who continued to promote their ideas after their death, such as Thomas Carr, Bernard Springett and Charles Merz; lady-masons, such as Aimee Bothwell Gosse and Marjorie Cecily Debenham, who did so much through their self-financed publications, the *Co- Mason* and *The Speculative Mason*, to clarify the ideas behind the Society; and those who did their best to preserve the history of the Society, such as J.D.Bing and the Rev'd. R.R.à-Ababrelton; those who remained 'in office' well into their latter years so as to keep the Society alive, such as R.F.B.Cross and John Lawrance; and those with the foresight to plan for the day when the Society would need a headquarters of its own, such as Derek Richard Stuckey and William Reginald Box; and those who took on the task of turning that vision into a reality, such as two long-serving Grand Treasurers, Nigel Willows and Roy Bedford and, of course, Peter Fotheringham, who is still serving the Society as Chairman of the Headquarters Premises Committee.

The lodgeroom in the new headquarters

There are too many to name them all, but some of their names are recorded in this book and it is hoped that, in the years to come, they will be remembered. In that connection it can only be hoped hoped that, if and when such a Toast is proposed, it will be to the Founders of the Society *and those who supported them.* They have left a landmark in free masonry for others to follow, and they deserve to be remembered.

APPENDIX A
Grand Master Masons of the Society

YEAR	1ST G.M.M.	2ND G.M.M.	3rd G.M.M.
1931	D. P. Hutchings	H. T. C. de la Fontaine	J. E. Whitty
1932	D. P. Hutchings	G. B. Cotton	F. M. Rickard
1933	F. E. Crate	J. E. Whitty	L. H. MacKelcken
1934	F. E. Crate	J. E. Whitty	G. B. Cotton
1935	F.E.Crate	J.E.Whitty	F.Cramphorn
1936	F.E.Crate	G.B.Cotton	A.W.Dentith
1937	F.E.Crate	G.B.Cotton	S.W.Wortley
1938	F.E.Crate	G.B.Cotton	E.B.Holmes
1939	F.E.Crate (r. 1940)	G.B.Cotton	E.B.Holmes
1940	R.F.B.Cross	G.B.Cotton	E.B.Holmes
1941	R.F.B.Cross	G.B.Cotton	E.B.Holmes
1942	R.F.B.Cross	G.B.Cotton	E.B.Holmes
1943	R.F.B.Cross	G.B.Cotton	E.B.Holmes
1944	R.F.B.Cross	G.B.Cotton	E.B.Holmes
1945	R.F.B.Cross	G.B.Cotton	E.B.Holmes
1946	R.F.B.Cross	A.W.Dentith	E.B.Holmes
1947	R.F.B.Cross	A.W.Dentith	E.B.Holmes
1948	R.F.B.Cross	A.W.Dentith	E.B.Holmes

YEAR	1ST G.M.M.	2ND G.M.M.	3rd G.M.M.
1949	R.F.B.Cross	A.W.Dentith	E.B.Holmes
1950	R.F.B.Cross	A.W.Dentith	E.B.Holmes
1951	R.F.B.Cross	A.W.Dentith	E.B.Holmes
1952	R.F.B.Cross	A.W.Dentith	E.B.Holmes (d. 1953)
1953	R.F.B.Cross	A.W.Dentith	F.J.R.Heath
1954	R.F.B.Cross	A.W.Dentith	G.H.R.Barham
1955	R.F.B.Cross	F.J.R.Heath (d. 1956)	T.W.S.Hills
1956	R.F.B.Cross	T.W.S.Hills	E.Le Fre
1957	R.F.B.Cross (d. 1958)	T.W.S.Hills	E.Le Fre
1958	T.W.S.Hills	L.F.Elvin	E.Le Fre
1959	T.W.S.Hills	L.F.Elvin	C.E.Coggan
1960	L.F.Elvin (acting)	E.Benjamin	R.J.L.Wilkinson
1961	L.F.Elvin (acting)	E.Benjamin	L.E.C.Peckover
1962	F. Stennett	L.F.Elvin	A.A.Murphy
1963	F. Stennett	L.F.Elvin	W.R.Hornby-Steer
1964	F. Stennett	L.F.Elvin	A.G.Rumbelow
1965	F. Stennett	L.F.Elvin	O. Anderson
1966	F. Stennett	L.F.Elvin	J.L. Jeffree

YEAR	1ST G.M.M.	2ND G.M.M.	3rd G.M.M.
1967	A.Moreton	L.F.Elvin	R.J.Hammond
1968	A.Moreton	L.F.Elvin	R.E.W.Large
1969	A.Moreton	L.F.Elvin	W.J.Wickham
1970	A.Moreton	L.F.Elvin	G.W.Hookham
1971	A.Moreton	L.F.Elvin	H.E.Pettingell
1972	L.F.Elvin	A.A.Murphy	F.Brough
1973	L.F.Elvin	A.A.Murphy	J.D.Bing
1974	L.F.Elvin	A.A.Murphy	F.Leistikow
1975	L.F.Elvin (d. 1976)	A.A.Murphy	L.J.Richardson
1976	A.A.Murphy	L.J.Richardson	J.H.Emerson
1977	A.A.Murphy	L.J.Richardson	A.B.Carver
1978	A.A.Murphy	L.J.Richardson	F.J.Gomm
1979	A.A.Murphy	J.H.Emerson	F.Wade-Cooper
1980	A.A.Murphy	J.H.Emerson	E.A.Gurnhill
1981	A.A.Murphy (d. 1981)	J.H.Emerson	A.E.Masters
1982	J.H.Emerson	F.J.Crow	J.L.Minard
1983	J.H.Emerson	F.J.Crow	H.A.Stokes
1984	J.H.Emerson	F.J.Crow	C.C.Corfield
1985	J.H.Emerson	F.J.Crow	E.G.G.White
1986	J.H.Emerson	F.J.Crow	G.T.Saxby
1987	J.H.Emerson	F.J.Crow	D.R.Stuckey

YEAR	1ST G.M.M.	2ND G.M.M.	3rd G.M.M.
1988	F.J.Crow	D.R.Stuckey	C.St.C.Crossley (d.1989, J.H.Berman
1989	F.J.Crow	D.R.Stuckey	A.Craddock
1990	F.J.Crow	D.R.Stuckey	H.T.Curlis
1991	D.R.Stuckey	A.Craddock	D.F.Walsh
1992	D.R.Stuckey	A.Craddock	A.S.Williams
1993	D.R.Stuckey	A.Craddock	W.A.Large
1994	D.R.Stuckey	A.Craddock	M.F.Hook
1995	D.R.Stuckey	A.S.Williams	S.C.Upton
1996	D.R.Stuckey	A.S.Williams	E.G.Hodkinson
1997	D.R.Stuckey	A.S.Williams	B.Burwood-Taylor
1998	A.Craddock	E.L.J.Smith	D.Baum
1999	A.Craddock	E.L.J.Smith	M.D.Arnold
2000	A.Craddock	E.L.J.Smith	C.B.Hasler
2001	A.Craddock	E.L.J.Smith	A.J.Keay
2002	A.Craddock	P.E.A.Fotheringham	N.T.G.Price
2003	A.Craddock	P.E.A.Fotheringham	J.S.Hay
2004	A.Craddock	P.E.A.Fotheringham	D.C.Kibble-Rees
2005	A.Craddock	D.Falconer	N.Willows

YEAR	1ST G.M.M.	2ND G.M.M.	3rd G.M.M.
2006	A.Craddock	D.Falconer	W.Summers
2007	A.Craddock	D.Falconer	D.B.Saunders
2008	A.Craddock	D.C.Kibble-Rees	D.C.Hooker
2009	A.Craddock	D.C.Kibble-Rees	J.W.Turner
2010	A.Craddock	D.C.Kibble-Rees	P.S.Hodgson
2011	N.A.Willows	B.Blanchard	G.T.Jones
2012	N.A.Willows	B.Blanchard (d. 2013) J. W. Turner	D.M.Edwards

r = resigned   d = died

PRO GRAND MASTER MASONS

1995-97   A.Craddock as Pro 2nd Grand Master Mason to cover for A.S.Williams*
2005-07   P.Fotheringham as Pro 2nd Grand Master Mason to cover for D.Falconer*
2012-13   J.W.Turner as Pro 2nd Grand Master Mason to cover for B.Blanchard during illness

* = resident in Australia

APPENDIX B

Principal Grand Officers

GRAND CLERK

1933	G. B. Cotton	1975	H. A. Stokes
1935	R. R. à-Abrabrelton	1982	D. R. Stuckey
1944	J. H. Hack	1988	W. R. Box
1950	C. E. Coggan	2000	D. C. Kibble-Rees
1959	J. E. Dodsworth	2004	B. Blanchard
1960	L. J. L. Boag	2011	P. Mycock
1963	L. J. Richardson		

GRAND REGISTRAR

1990	R. S. Filbey	2004	P. H. Davis
1992	N. T. G. Price	2008	P. Mycock
1999	B. F. Muir	2011	B. W. Price
2000	B. Blanchard	2012	S. A. Mighall

GRAND BURSAR

1976 F. J. Crow
1981 M. Johnson
1990 G.S.Cope
1993 J.S.Hay

1998 B.F.Muir
1999 D.C.Kibble-Rees
2001 A.M.J.Brown
2005 D.B.F. Burt

GRAND TREASURER

1933 P. W. Morehen
1940 H.L.Howard
1950 N.Gutteridge
1960 C.E.Goddard
1963 J.L.Jeffree
1966 K.D.L.Bale
1967 J.L.Jeffree
1971 J.H.Emerson

1976 H.Newman
1977 J.H.Emerson
1979 H.Newman
1983 A.B.Stephenson
1985 T.J.Lewis
1991 N.T.G.Price
1992 N.A.Willows
2001 R.J.Bedford

G.M.Ms' S.I.Wk.

1990 B. Clarke
2002 R. G. Fretten
2005 J. J. Field

GRAND OUTSIDE GUARD

1988 G. H. Vincent

1999 B. A. Bailes

2004 E. H. Last

2011 T. Thomson

GRAND J

1967 W.B. Hodgson

1968 A.B. Carver

1981 D. Walker

1982 E.G.G. White

1984 H.T. Curlis

1990 J.M. Tuckey

1993 R.F. Heron

1996 M.D. Arnold

1998 M.D. Legg

2000 A. Alvey

2003 D. Lower

2005 A. Alvey

2007 K.W. Henderson

2009 B.A. Bailes

2012 B.W. Price

GRAND B

1967 J.R. Hatcher   1993 G.S. Cope
1968 R.B. Dinsdale   1996 R.H. Weeks
1971 R.J. Knott   1998 D.W. Southgate
1975 F.J. Gomm   2002 D.W.B. Bale
1981 S. Wilkinson   2003 P.S. Hodgson
1982 D. Walker   2009 W. Beard
1990 M.F. Hook

GRAND LIBRARIAN

1993 S. Robinson   2003 J. Shaw
1996 R.L.W. White   2005 V.A.T. Brown
1999 R. Bavin

APPENDIX C

The Regions

The Regions shown are those as at 1st January 2013 and they are listed in alphabetical order. Their Deputy Grand Master Masons (who also act as Senior Passed Masters in a VI° lodge) are listed in the order of their appointment. Patents of appointment are normally for five years.

AUSTRALIA CENTRAL

DGMM&SPM	YEAR APPOINTED
D. M. Hedges	1999
W. R. Harding	2011
ASSEMBLAGES	LOCATION
Chirnside Mansion	Preston, Victoria
Eureka Quarries	Ardeer, Victoria
Invergowrie Homestead	Melbourne, Victoria
Murrindale Park	Warragul, Victoria

AUSTRALIA EASTERN

DGMM&SPM	YEAR APPOINTED
D. H. B. Falconer	1995
F. Jefferies	2005
R. J. Adam	2010

ASSEMBLAGES	LOCATION
Fort Denison	Willoughby, NSW
Innisfallen Castle	Concord West, NSW

AUSTRALIA NORTH EASTERN

DGMM&SPM	YEAR APPOINTED
D. P. Dezentje	2003
R. G. Hodges	2009

ASSEMBLAGES	LOCATION
Bishopsbourne	Brisbane, Queensland
Customs House	Townsville, Queensland

AUSTRALIA SOUTH

DGMM&SPM	YEAR APPOINTED
H. R. Goatham	2005
B. J. A. Eves	2011

ASSEMBLAGES	LOCATION
Bonython Hall	Lower Mitcham, SA
Toll House	Lower Mitcham, SA

AUSTRALIA WEST

DGMM&SPM	YEAR APPOINTED
E. M.Adams	1997
I. Munachen	2009
W. F. Eccles	2012

ASSEMBLAGES	LOCATION
Round House	Fremantle, WA
Shentons Mill	East Perth, WA

CANADA

DGMM&SPM	YEAR APPOINTED
G. T. Jones	2001
A. J. Seguin	2005
M. Sastre	2010

ASSEMBLAGE	LOCATION
St. Lawrence Seaway	Ottawa

CHILTERN AND THAMES

DGMM&SPM	YEAR APPOINTED
E. R. Bunn	2004
R. Machin	2008
N. A. Willows	2009
J. L. Jarvis	2011

ASSEMBLAGES	LOCATION
Bentley Priory	Harrow
Burnham Abbey	Beaconsfield
Hampton Court Palace	Twickenham
Woburn Abbey	Leighton Buzzard

CITY OF LONDON

DGMM&SPM	YEAR APPOINTED
P. E. A. Fotheringham	1996
E. R. Bunn	2002
R. Bavin	2004
B. A. Vickers	2008

ASSEMBLAGES	LOCATION
Guildhall	City of London
Mansion House	City of London
St. Pauls	City of London

EAST ANGLIAN COUNTIES

DGMM&SPM	YEAR APPOINTED
B. Clarke	1987
P. E. A. Fotheringham	1990
K. Ansell	1995
D. B. Saunders	2000
R. G. Fretten	2005

ASSEMBLAGES	LOCATION
Castle Acre	Diss
Edmundsbury Abbey	Bury St. Edmunds
Friars Walk Chelmersforde	Southend-on-Sea

EAST MIDLAND COUNTIES

DGMM&SPM	YEAR APPOINTED
P. E. A. Fotheringham	1995
E. W. Bamford	2000
P. M. Collins	2012

ASSEMBLAGES	LOCATION
Ancaster Quarry	Louth
Breedon & Cloud Hill Quarry	Lutterworth
Collyweston Quarry	Rushden
Eaton Socon Church	Eaton Socon

FRANCE

DGMM&SPM	YEAR APPOINTED
P. Jaillet	2006

ASSEMBLAGES	LOCATION
Carthusians Quarry	Paris
Mount of Martyrs Quarry	Paris

HONG KONG AND THE FAR EAST

DGMM&SPM	YEAR APPOINTED
P. R. Whitmore	2009

ASSEMBLAGES	LOCATION
St. John's	Hong Kong
Tung Chung Fort	Hong Kong

IBERIA

DGMM&SPM	YEAR APPOINTED
F. B. Capes	2005
B. Blanchard	2006
B. Ashcroft	2009

ASSEMBLAGES	LOCATION
Rojales Quarry	Alicante
Torres De Serrano	Callosa de'En Sarria

NEW ZEALAND

DGMM&SPM	YEAR APPOINTED
R. H. Weekes	1993
A. J. Keay	1997
G. J. Davies	2000
H. D. L. Morgans	2004
R. J. Sutherland	2009

ASSEMBLAGES	LOCATION
Albert Barracks	Auckland
Belmont Quarries	Petone
Halswell Quarry	Christchurch
Napier Quarries	Napier
Wakefield Quarry	Nelson

NORTHERN COUNTIES

DGMM&SPM	YEAR APPOINTED
C. Warham	2005

ASSEMBLAGES	LOCATION
Church Quarry	Chester-Le-Street
Stranton Church	Hartlepool
Woodhorn Church	Ashington

NORTH EASTERN COUNTIES

DGMM&SPM	YEAR APPOINTED
W. Summers	2000
D. Fox	2006
G. F. Setterfield	2011

ASSEMBLAGES	LOCATION
Bolton Abbey	Leeds
Guisborough Priory	Guisborough
Kirstall Abbey	York
Meaux Abbey	Beverley

NORTHERN EUROPE

DGMM&SPM	YEAR APPOINTED
D. C. Kibble-Rees	2006
P. Noel	2008

ASSEMBLAGES	LOCATION
St. Peter's Quarry	Brussels

NORTH MIDLAND COUNTIES

DGMM&SPM	YEAR APPOINTED
W. Summers	2000
R. S. Moss	2006

ASSEMBLAGES	LOCATION

NORTH MIDLAND COUNTIES

Beauchief Abbey	Sheffield
Duffield Castle	Belper
Linby Quarry	Mansfield
Nottingham Castle	Long Eaton

NORTHERN STATES OF INDIA

DGMM&SPM	YEAR APPOINTED
S. J. Hindes	2009
A. S. Vakil	2012

ASSEMBLAGES	LOCATION
Castella de Aguada	Mumbai
Gateway of India	Mumbai

NORTH WESTERN COUNTIES

DGMM&SPM	YEAR APPOINTED
J. E. Glover	1989
D. F. Walsh	1992
F. A. Starkey	1998
F. E. Hargreaves	2003

ASSEMBLAGES	LOCATION
Saint Helen	Manchester
St. Cuthbert	Ormskirk
St. Werburgh	Wallasey

SOUTH AFRICA

DGMM&SPM	YEAR APPOINTED
A Spencer	2011

ASSEMBLAGES	LOCATION
Begane Quarry	Durban
Cape Town Castle	Cape Town
Northwards House	Johannesburg

SOUTH AMERICA

DGMM&SPM	YEAR APPOINTED
J. G. Mendoza Quiroga	2011

ASSEMBLAGES	LOCATION
Basilica De San Francisco	Bolivia
Canteras De San Jose	Bolivia
Catedral De Nuestra Senora De La Paz	Bolivia
Catedral De Sao Paulo	Brazil
Le Paz Quarry	Bolivia
Santa Casa De Misericordia	Brazil
Solare Dos Andradas	Brazil

SOUTHERN COUNTIES

DGMM&SPM	YEAR APPOINTED
W. A. Large	1988
B. H. Burwood-Taylor	1993
N. A. Willows	1996
A. Mitchell-Fyffe	2005
R. J. Bridger	2010

ASSEMBLAGES	LOCATION
Bliss Mill	Woodstock
Loddon Bridge	Wokingham
Winchester Castle	Winchester

SOUTH EAST ASIA

DGMM&SPM	YEAR APPOINTED
K. C. Cheah	2009

ASSEMBLAGES	LOCATION
Fort Canning	Singapore
Kellie's Castle	Perak
Twin Towers	Kuala Lumpur

SOUTH EASTERN COUNTIES

DGMM&SPM	YEAR APPOINTED
S. C. Upton	1988
E. L. J. Smith	1994
R. H. Button	1998
H. Small	2005
J. Knox	2008

ASSEMBLAGES	LOCATION
Bodiam Castle	Peacehaven
Chislehurst Caves	Bromley
Leeds Castle	Gillingham
Market Cross	Chichester
Nonsuch Palace	Sutton
Reculver Towers	Whitstable

SOUTHERN STATES OF INDIA

DGMM&SPM	YEAR APPOINTED
K. Madhavan	2008

ASSEMBLAGES	LOCATION
Fort St. George	Chennai
Shore Temple	Chennai
Thiruvananthapuram Quarry	Thiruvananthapuram

SOUTH WESTERN COUNTIES

DGMM&SPM	YEAR APPOINTED
M. A. Tapley	1990
N. T. G. Price	1993
T. J. Barnett	1998
D. W. B. Bale	2003

ASSEMBLAGES	LOCATION
Berry Head Quarry	Brixham
Bodiniel Quarry	Bodmin
Purbeck Quarries	Wareham

TASMANIA

DGMM&SPM	YEAR APPOINTED
D. M. Hedges	1999
P. Sargeant	2003
M. C. Frymyer	2003
I. C. Blair	2006

ASSEMBLAGES	LOCATION
Barton Mill	Newstead
Highfield House	Burnie
Salamanca Quarry	Glenorchy

UNITED STATES OF AMERICA

DGMM&SPM	YEAR APPOINTED
M. D. Dupee	2010

ASSEMBLAGES	LOCATION
Bryn Athyn Quarry	Allentown, PA
Bull Run Quarry	Winchester, VA
Solar White Quarry	Monroe, NC
Texas State Capitol	San Antonio, TX
Trinity Church	New York, NY

WEST ANGLIAN COUNTIES

DGMM&SPM	YEAR APPOINTED
P. E. A. Fotheringham	1995
A. H. Turney	2000
B. F. Muir	2003
I. D. L. Bany	2008

ASSEMBLAGES	LOCATION
Royston Priory	Royston
St. Albans Abbey	St. Albans
Totternhoe Quarries	Dunstable
Waltham Abbey	Cheshunt

WESTERN COUNTIES & SOUTH WALES

DGMM&SPM	YEAR APPOINTED

WESTERN COUNTIES & SOUTH WALES

K. Adkins	1995
F. Gabb	1997
I. S. Parry	2001
A. M. J. Brown	2006
G. S. Gubb	2008
A. P. Beaumont	2012
ASSEMBLAGES	LOCATION
Box Tunnel	Melksham
Burnham Lighthouse	Burnham-on-Sea
Cabot Tower	Bristol
Cardiff Castle	Newport
Ludgershall Castle	Ludgershall
Theoc Abbey	Tewkesbury

WEST MIDLAND COUNTIES

DGMM&SPM	YEAR APPOINTED
D. R. Boston	1996
D. C. Hooker	2002
D. M. Edwards	2007
S. I. Edwards	2011
ASSEMBLAGES	LOCATION
Dudley Castle	Birmingham

WEST MIDLAND COUNTIES

Kenilworth Castle	Warwick
Wrekin Quarries	Wellington
Weoley Castle	Birmingham

WESTMINSTER

DGMM&SPM	YEAR APPOINTED
J. Lawrance	1932
E. Benjamin	1961
F. H. Crow	1977
P. W. Lonnon	1982
J. H. Berman	1988
P. E. A. Fotheringham	1989
A. G. Davies	1991
B. Clarke	1995
D. Alexander	2003
S. M. Ayres	2008

ASSEMBLAGES	LOCATION
Abbey	London
Channel Row	London

APPENDIX D

The Assemblages

Unlike Craft lodges, Operative Assemblages do not use numbers as part of their titles. If they did, Channel Row Assemblage would be classified as a "Time Immemorial" lodge. They take their names from important man-made structures and are listed according to their date of constitution.

NAME OF ASSEMBLAGE	CONSTITUTED
Channel Row	21 May 1913
Abbey	9 February 1943
Kirkstall Abbey	14 April 1962
Purbeck Quarries	17 May 1969
St. Werburgh	22 July 1972
Friars Walk Chelmersforde	28 July 1973
Saint Helen	2 August 1977
Bodiam Castle	9 August 1977
Dudley Castle	8 July 1980
Berry Head Quarry	25 June 1981
Loddon Bridge	5 September 1983
Nonsuch Palace	26 June 1986
Castle Acre	29 July 1986

NAME OF ASSEMBLAGE	**CONSTITUTED**
Leeds Castle	29 September 1986
Winchester Castle	18 April 1988
Waltham Abbey	23 May 1988
Bodiniel Quarry	26 October 1988
Chirnside Mansion	3 April 1989
Eureka Quarries	5 April 1989
Innisfallen Castle	5 April 1989
Shentons Mill	6 April 1989
Bishopsbourne	7 April 1989
Bonython Hall	7 April 1989
Bliss Mill	18 May 1991
Round House	1 October 1991
Invergowrie Homestead	4 October 1991
Murrindale Park	5 October 1991
Belmont Quarries	12 October 1991
Albert Barracks	14 October 1991
Stranton Church	14 December 1991
Beauchief Abbey	11 January 1992
St. Pauls	20 April 1993
Royston Priory	13 September 1993
St. Cuthbert	12 November 1993

NAME OF ASSEMBLAGE	CONSTITUTED
Duffield Castle	20 July 1994
Ancaster Quarry	15 December 1994
Cardiff Castle	29 July 1995
Fort Denison	13 October 1995
Halswell Quarry	14 October 1995
Napier Quarries	19 October 1995
Woodhorn Church	4 November 1995
Collyweston Quarry	18 November 1995
Box Tunnel	29 November 1995
Kenilworth Castle	29 February 1996
Carthusians Quarry	7 September 1996
Barton Mill	3 May 1997
Salamanca Quarry	4 May 1997
Customs House	8 May 1997
Totternhoe Quarries	21 August 1997
Torres de Serrano	18 April 1998
St. Lawrence Seaway	10 July 1998
St. Peter's Quarry	26 September 2000
Guildhall	16 December 2000
Burnham Abbey	12 January 2002
Bentley Priory	16 January 2002

NAME OF ASSEMBLAGE	**CONSTITUTED**
Market Cross	17 July 2002
Wrekin Quarries	3 December 2002
King Solomon's Quarries	10 February 2003
Highfield House	24 May 2003
Wakefield Quarry	28 May 2003
Edmundsbury Abbey	30 June 2003
Hampton Court Palace	3 July 2003
Breedon & Cloud Hill	19 February 2004
Woburn Abbey	1 July 2004
Guisborough Priory	22 November 2004
Linby Quarry	30 November 2004
Toll House	14 March 2005
Rojales Quarry	31 May 2005
Mount of Martyrs Quarry	9 July 2005
Burnham Lighthouse	30 March 2006
Ludgershall Castle	24 August 2006
Weoley Castle	22 March 2007
Mansion House	29 May 2007
Bolton Abbey	25 August 2007
Reculver Towers	12 September 2007
Theoc Abbey	28 February 2008

NAME OF ASSEMBLAGE	CONSTITUTED
Meaux Abbey	16 September 2008
Gateway of India	2 October 2008
Castella de Aguada	3 October 2008
Fort St. George	8 October 2008
Nottingham Castle	21 October 2008
Bryn Athyn Quarry	29 November 2008
Twin Towers	15 February 2009
Santa Casa de Misericordia	27 September 2009
Catedral de Sao Paulo	29 September 2009
Solar dos Andradas	29 September 2009
St. Johns	31 October 2009
Tung Chung Fort	1 November 2009
Solar White Quarry	15 February 2010
Texas State Capitol	16 February 2010
Trinity Church	17 February 2010
Chislehurst Caves	16 June 2010
Begane Quarry	15 August 2010
Northwards House	20 August 2010
Cape Town Castle	25 August 2010
Kellie's Castle	30 October 2010
Fort Canning	31 October 2010

NAME OF ASSEMBLAGE	CONSTITUTED
Cabot Tower	9 November 2010
Eaton Socon Church	22 November 2010
Thiruvanathapuram Quarry	12 March 2011
Shore Temple	15 March 2011
Church Quarry	16 July 2011
St. Albans Quarry	29 September 2011
Bull Run Quarry	13 February 2012
La Paz Quarry	20 March 2012
Basilica de San Francisco	21 March 2012
C'dral de Nuestra Senora de la Paz	23 March 2012
Canteras de San Jose	24 March 2012

APPENDIX E

Recipients of the Grand Master Masons' Order of Service to Operative Masonry

2003	Rt. W. Bro. Edward Laurence Joseph Smith, VII°
2008	Rt. W. Bro. Peter Ernest Albert Fotheringham, VII°
2009	Rt. W. Bro. Paul Herbert Davis, VII°
2012	Rt. W. Bro. Brian Blanchard, VII°

INDEX

	Page(s)
à-Ababrelton, Rev. R. R.	14,34,35,50,53,55,92
Antient Drama	38,70
Arms of the Society	23.34
ASSEMBLAGES	120
Abbey	51,87,119,120
Albert Barracks	61,110,121
Ancaster Quarry	108,122
Barton Mill	116,122
Basilica de San Francisco	113,125
Beauchief Abbey	112,121
Begane Quarry	113,124
Belmont Quarries	61,110,124
Bentley Priory	107,122
Berry Head Quarry	58,116,120
Bishopsbourne	60,105,121
Bliss Mill	114,121
Bodiam Castle	58,63,115,120
Bodiniel Quarry	58,116,121
Bolton Abbey	111,123
Bonython Hall	60,105,121
Box Tunnel	118,122
Breedon & Cloud Hill	108,123
Bryn Athyn Quarry	117,124
Bull Run Quarry	117,125
Burnham Abbey	107,122
Burnham Lighthouse	107,122

Cabot Tower	118,124
Canteras de San Jose	113,125
Cardiff Castle	118,122
Cape Town Castle	113,124
Carthusians Quarry	109,122
Castella de Aguada	112,124
Castle Acre	58,108,120
Catedral de Sao Paulo	113,124
Catedral de Nuestra de la Paz	113,125
Channel Row	5,26,36,48,49,52,62,85,119,120
Chirnside Mansion	60,104,121
Chislehurst Caves	115,124
Church Quarry	110,125
Collyweston Quarry	108,122
Customs House	105,122
Dudley Castle	58,118,120
Duffield Castle	112,121
Eaton Socon Church	108,125
Edmundsbury Abbey	58,108,123
Eureka Quarries	60,104,121
Fort Canning	114,124
Fort Denison	105,122
Fort St.George	115,124
Friars Walk,Chelmersforde	50,51,57,58,108,120
Gateway of India	112,124
Guildhall	107,122
Guisborough Priory	111,123
Halswell Quarry	110,122
Hampton Court Palace	107,123
Highfield House	116,123

Innisfallen Castle	60,105,121
Invergowrie Homestead	61,104,121
Kellie's Castle	114,124
Kenilworth Castle	119,122
King Solomon's Quarries	123
Kirkstall Abbey	52,56,111,120
La Paz Quarry	113,125
Leeds Castle	58,115,120
Linby Quarry	112,123
Loddon Bridge	58,114,120
Ludgershall Castle	118,123
Mansion House	107,123
Market Cross	115,122
Meaux Abbey	111,123
Mount of Martyrs	109,123
Murrindale Park	61,104,121
Napier Quarries	110,122
Nonsuch Palace	58,115,120
Northwards House	113,124
Nottingham Castle	112,124
Purbeck Quarries	56,116,120
Reculver Towers	115,123
Rojales Quarry	109,123
Round House	61,106,121
Royston Priory	117,121
Saint Helen	58,112,120
Salamanca Quarry	116,122
St. Albans Abbey	117,125
St. Cuthbert	112,122
St. John's	109,124

St. Lawrence Seaway	106,122
St. Paul's	107,121
St. Peter's Quarry	58,111,122
St. Werburgh	57,112,120
Santa Casa de Misericordia	113,124
Shenton's Mill	60,106,121
Shore Temple	115,125
Solar dos Andradas	113,124
Solar White Quarry	117,124
Stranton Church	110,121
Texas State Capitol	117,124
Theoc Abbey	118,123
Thiruvanathapuram Quarry	115,125
Toll House	105,123
Torres de Serrano	109,122
Totternhoe Quarries	117,122
Trinity Church	117,124
Tung Chung Fort	109,124
Twin Towers	114,124
Wakefield Quarry	110,123
Waltham Abbey	58,117,121
Weoley Castle	119,123
Winchester Castle	58,114121
Woodhorn Church	110,122
Wrekin Quarries	119,123
Bedford,R.	93,101
Bijou Theatre	29,33,35
Bing, J.D.	35,36,55,92,97
Blanchard,B.	99,100,126

Bothwell-Gosse, J.A.	41,42,43,44,45,49,92
Bowes, A.	15,17,22
Box, W.R.	62,63,65,88,93,100
Bridge, G.E.W.	40
Buckmaster, F.H.	16,31,33
Carr, Dr.T.	15,17,26,31,32,34,35,69,74,83,92
Coat of Arms	23,34
Cockburn, Sir J.A.	43,46
Co-Masons	41,42,43,45
Court of Assistants	37,38,39
Craddock, A.	88,89,98,99
Crate, Rev.F.E.	50,95
Cryer, Rev.N.B.	9,13,27,52,55,67
Dat, B.	10,27
Davis, P.H.	100,126
Debenham, M.C.	44,45,92
Elvin, L.F.	53,54,96,97
Fontaine, H.T.C. de L.	39,47
Footing Corner Stone Fund	63,87
Fotheringham, P.E.A.	64,93,98,99,107,108,117,119,126
Gauges	72,73
George, A.E.	16,31
Godward, H.N.	16,31,39
Gorham, Major A.	15,17,21,27,31,32,35,40
Grand Master Masons	38,74,85,86,95
Grand Officers	62, 85,100
Grant, R.B.	15,17,23,24,44,70
Green, P.H.I.	59,61
Hasluck, P.	16,30,31,33,35
Henderson, K.	59,60,61,68,102

Hexagonal pedestals	75
Indenture	76
Keys	76
Lawrence, J.	40,54,92
Liberal Arts & Sciences	77
Jabal	76
Masonic Study Society	42,45,46,47,48,49
Nicholls, H.	16,31,35
Order of Service to Operative Masonry	126
Orientation of Lodges	78
Nourse, W.J.C.	31
Pollock, Rt.Hon. Sir F.	39,48
Powell, J.	16,33,35
Purser, J.G.	15,17,23
Regalia	79
Religion	79
REGIONS	104
Australia Central	104
Australia Eastern	105
Australia North Eastern	105
Australia South	105
Australia West	106
Canada	106
Chiltern and Thames	107
City of London	107
East Anglian Counties	108
East Midland Counties	108
France	109
Hong Kong and the Far East	109
Iberia	109

New Zealand	110
Northern Counties	110
Northern States of India	112
North Eastern Counties	111
Northern Europe	111
North Midland Counties	111
North Western Counties	112
South Africa	113
South America	113
South East Asia	114
South Eastern Counties	115
Southern Counties	114
Southern States of India	115
South Western Counties	116
Tasmania	116
United States of America	117
West Anglian Counties	117
Western Coiunties & South Wales	117
West Midland Counties	118
Westminster	13,33,,34,35,36,39,54,119
Reynolds, E.V.	16,31
Rods, GMMs	75
Seven-degree system	80
Sitwell, Brigadier General W.H.	40
Smith, E.L.J.	98,126
Springett, B.H.	39,43,44,47,49,92
Stitt, Rev.S.S.	16,17,21,44
Stretton, C.E. 5,6,7,12,15,17,20,22,23,24,25,26,27,34,36,42,44,92	
Stuckey, D.R.	61,62,63,64,65,87,93,97,98,100
Swastika	72

Super Intendent of Work	81,82
Truncheons	82
Walker, Colonel H.	16,31,32,35,38
Waite, A.E.	47
Ward, J.S.M.	46
Wilkinson, R.J.	53,55,96
Willows, N.A.	4,89,93,98,99,101
Yarker, J.	15,17,18,19,20,22,42,44,92